AF838128

INSURANCE SOLUTIONS,

Plan Well—Live Better: A Workbook for People with a Chronic Disease or Disability

LAURA D. COOPER, ESQ.

Demos

Demos Medical Publishing, Inc., 386 Park Avenue South,
New York, New York 10016

Library of Congress Cataloging-in-Publication Data

Cooper, Laura, 1956–
Insurance solutions, plan well—live better : a workbook for people with a chronic disease or disability / Laura Cooper.
p. cm.
Includes bibliographical references.
ISBN 1-888799-44-7 (pbk.)
1. Insurance, Health. 2. Chronically ill—Long-term care—Finance. 3. Medical care, Cost of. I. Title.

RA411.C665 2002
368.38′2 dc21

2001058443

Made in the United States of America

Disclaimer

Dedication

This book is dedicated to my mother, Grace B. Cooper, who was my lifeline and remains my daily inspiration. It is also dedicated to three brave people: Brian Harnetiaux, Leona Dater, and Dr. William Bond, all of Spokane, Washington, without whose collective vision, dedication, assistance, and determination I would never have been in a position to write this book.

Acknowledgments

I would like to acknowledge the assistance of a number of people who were critical to the development and completion of this book. Dr. Diana M. Schneider publisher of Demos Medical Publishing, Inc., was instrumental in encouraging me to develop this topic into a book. Both she and her editor Joan Wolk have worked hard to produce this volume, and deserve an enormous amount of credit for having the vision to understand its importance and for guiding me in its craftsmanship along the way. I also wish to acknowledge the great support and influence of Dr. Nancy Holland and Pamela Cavallo of the National Multiple Sclerosis Society's national office. They have struggled with these topics on behalf of people with multiple sclerosis for decades, and have provided both insight and immeasurable amounts of support for me for the last ten years while I have developed the knowledge base for the writing of this book. I would also like to thank Diane Afes, a member of the staff of the National Capital Chapter of the National Multiple Sclerosis Society, for providing the initial inspiration about a decade ago to encourage me to develop this resource. Here it is, finally, Diane!

CONTENTS

INTRODUCTION

What the Financial Planners Didn't Tell You

If you are like most people, you were not sufficiently financially prepared for significant long-term disability or chronic illness when it occurred. Even most people who *think* they are prepared often discover—to their dismay—that they are woefully unprepared. To compound matters, most financial professionals are not well-versed in the complex web of considerations necessary for thorough health insurance planning in the face of chronic illness or disability. For example, most financial planners fail to include comprehensive planning that takes into account the almost certain loss of employer-sponsored health coverage after leaving work due to illness or disability.

At a minimum, a chronic illness or other long-term disability will inject uncertainty into your social and financial future. For example, consider what might happen if you are the primary breadwinner in your family and your employer-sponsored health insurance provides your family's coverage. If you become too ill to work, you may jeopardize your *family's* entire health insurance package. And, while you are in this situation, you will somehow need to provide alternative income for the time you are not working, including finding income supplements for additional expenses resulting from your disability. After your diagnosis it will be difficult to increase your life insurance to provide ample financial security for your loved ones. Even if you were able to return to work and were able to obtain adequate health insurance coverage from your employer or elsewhere, you might not be as productive as you were before your disability occurred. Your lack of productivity would diminish the income you could garner. All of these possibilities are daunting, to say the least. If you planned for all of them, you might be able to salvage whatever lifestyle you had before your illness occurred. If you adequately planned for none or only part of them and had to endure a significant illness for a substantial period of time, your quality of life—and that of your family—would probably be diminished as a result.

Needless to say, if you have a chronic illness, you need to find some way to safeguard your assets from the risk of potential extraordinary disability-related costs. Even if you attempt to create a financial plan to minimize the risk of significant losses from a chronic illness, you will probably discover that there is a dearth of information about *how* to plan for a chronic illness. You will undoubtedly also discover that most professional financial planners are ill-equipped to handle complex disability, life, and health insurance issues for a person with a chronic illness.

This is partly because financial planning becomes fundamentally different from ordinary individual financial planning after you have been diagnosed with a chronic illness.[1] If you are middle class and your chronic illness becomes severe enough to require long-term services (especially while you are still relatively young), you cannot normally expect to accrue enough wealth to pay for those extraordinarily expensive long-term services. Instead, you will probably have to develop alternative financial and estate plans that take explicit account of potential government benefits to provide a funding mechanism for such services.

Other special considerations need to be given to your financial plan after you have been diagnosed with a chronic illness. First, you must take into account the possibility that you could lose your employer-sponsored insurance benefits if you must retire due to disability.[2] Because of this, you should make sure that you have adequate non–employment-based insurance before your employment ceases.[3] Second, your entire financial plan must also be adjusted to take into account the increased likelihood that you will prematurely cease employment due to chronic illness.

For all of these reasons, you should deem it necessary to engage in significant and thorough insurance protection planning, taking into account the specific possibility of chronic illness or disability. The object of protection planning is to find ways to lessen the risks of your chronic illness; e.g., to make yourself and your loved ones as "bulletproof" as possible, given whatever unpleasant surprises your health conditions might bring. Because you could be financially responsible for enormous expenses in the face of an uninsured serious illness, planning in advance with insurance is a logical alternative to paying the bills afterward.

In this way, you should think of insurance as really just a means of *controlling* your risk. In other words, rather than risking all the financial consequences of disability, you instead pay a premium and transfer some of the risk for the financial consequences to an insurance company. Of course, the more likely it is that the financial consequences will be significant, the less likely it is that the insurance company will want to undertake them by selling you a policy. Thus,

---

[1] Although this difference exists in actual practice, the difference is not based upon a principled rationale. Ordinary financial planning should as a matter of course consider the possibility of accruing significant chronic illness or disability. The level of planning for these possibilities by most planners can at best be described as superficial, and certainly not comprehensive enough to provide any really thorough analysis of insurance issues.

[2] A key provision of the federal 1996 Health Insurance Portability and Accountability Act (HIPAA) ensures "portability" of protection by guaranteeing individual coverage upon leaving an employer group. Nevertheless, a recent U.S. General Accounting Office report indicates that people who try to exercise their rights under this law are often charged premiums far higher than standard. This has had the effect of preventing them from purchasing coverage. In addition, some insurers are reported to have created sales disincentives for their agents by refusing to pay them commissions for policy sales to applicants with preexisting conditions. Even if your employer continues to provide benefits during disability retirement, you need to take into account the possibility that your employer will not honor its commitment—or be around to do so—decades into the future.

[3] Later I will explain why—despite the financial advice of many planners and tax experts—it is advisable to seek insurance that is not employer-sponsored.

the most important types of insurance for a person with a disability are, unfortunately, precisely the types of insurance that become scarce following diagnosis of a significant disability or chronic medical condition.

In fact, many of the insurance strategies that work best for people with chronic illnesses are *counterintuitive* and nontraditional, precisely because a person with a chronic illness is essentially playing a "cat and mouse" game with insurance companies. The goal, of course, is to find and purchase something that a profitable insurance company would not generally want you to have. Consequently, most of the strategies incorporated in this workbook allow you to "hide in plain sight" within a larger pool of people who have insurance, so that the profits from the larger pool enable the insurance company to turn a tidy profit even with the increased risk your illness brings to the pool. This workbook also suggests strategies that may be used to help you obtain coverage if you find that your health condition has precluded you from obtaining adequate insurance through traditional sources. You will even find a few strategies that, when employed in the proper circumstances, can help you *augment your income* in addition to your insurance portfolio.

Insurance Solutions is a workbook for adults with chronic illnesses or disabilities to use either alone or with other people (such as with a family or support group). It contains exercises, worksheets, checklists, and list of resources for further study. Its objectives are to help you: (1) catalog your current illness-relevant insurance information; (2) evaluate the comprehensiveness and quality of the insurance products you own; and (3) improve your illness-relevant basic insurance portfolios. Most people with significant chronic illnesses or disabilities have difficulty obtaining their necessary life, disability, health or long-term care insurance *at any price.* Unlike other insurance planning sources, therefore, the primary focus of this workbook is explicitly *not* to cut insurance costs.

It is important to note that this workbook does not deal with the complete subject of protection, financial, or life planning. It is limited only to protection planning with those insurance products that are likely to be most significantly affected following a diagnosis of a chronic illness or disability and only assists you in developing a basic plan. A more thorough plan encompasses a complex methodical sequential series of steps and is part of an overall financial plan. The steps in creating this larger plan include: determining where you are financially; setting goals; developing the plan; keeping simple records; making an informal budget; dealing with shortfalls, credit, and debt; and reviewing your progress. Within that process, a financial planner would assess your total assets, liabilities, and future income potential, and then use that information to determine your best options for meeting future needs and wants. A comprehensive financial planning process may include the assessment of a myriad of financial options, including insurance, annuities, pensions, home equity, and the availability of government benefits. This workbook can serve very well to augment assessment of insurance contained in an overall financial plan. Certified financial planners and lawyers may be valuable in sorting through the options and identifying the possible legal and tax consequences of various choices and choice combinations. Additional consumer resources on insurance planning (including financial planning) are listed at the end of this workbook. To assist you with the language of insurance, Appendix 3 contains a glossary of terms to which you may wish to refer.

■ KEY CONCEPTS

So where should you begin? Before you dive into the following exercises, you should first become familiar with some key concepts.

1. Everybody Should Plan

Contrary to popular myth, planning is not necessary only for the wealthy. The less you have, the *more important* it is that you plan wisely in order to deploy your scarce resources in the most effective manner possible. Similarly, the greater the possibility that you will have large expenses from illness or unemployment, the more you need to make sure you are adequately prepared for them.

2. Risk Planning Principle

The most important principle of risk planning is that you should plan for the *worst* scenario. If you are prepared to meet the most difficult challenges head-on, you will not have to cope with devastating financial loss exactly when you are least equipped for it.

3. Everybody Has a Plan

Whether you realize it or not, you already have a plan. The "plan" may be simply to take things as they come, to live from paycheck to paycheck, and to presume therefore that you will not get sick, old, or disabled. Whenever it occurs, some form of planning is always better than no plan whatsoever.

4. It Matters Who the Underwriting Insurance Company Is

Financial protection plans involving insurance products are developed for the long term. Insurance that you purchase today may not be needed for years or even decades. It is important that the dollars you spend today will make that protection available for you *when you need it*. You must therefore make sure that the insurance companies or other entities that provide your insurance, such as an employer or fraternal association (with whom you are entrusting your future), are financially sound[4] and will remain available to you during the time you will need their protection. A company needs to be financially sound enough to pay claims not only now but also in future decades when you need to count on your benefits.[5] As you grow older and your health changes, you may discover that you can no longer purchase the same benefits that you could purchase at a younger age when you were healthier. Thus, you need to regard the decisions you make now as permanent, life-long choices, because it is impossible to predict when illness or disability will occur that will limit the market options for purchasing insurance you have as a healthy indivdual.

[4] So serious is the problem of failing insurance companies that in some states doctors and hospitals require their patients to agree in writing to pay a bill on which their insurers default.

[5] See page 5 for information on obtaining insurer financial strength ratings.

For example, if you choose to use your employer's plan as your protection, you should regard your employment (and your employer's coverage) as permanent, life-long employment. If you change jobs after you get older or your health deteriorates, you may discover that you cannot obtain adequate life, health, or disability coverage *even with your employer's coverage.* If you are not guaranteed that coverage by a contract with your employer (including *cost* and *content of coverage*), the type and cost of your protection will be subject to the discretion of your employer.[6]

The 1996 Health Insurance Portability and Accountability Act (HIPAA) provides that in many cases you and your family will be entitled to coverage under a new employer's plan after changing jobs without exclusion for preexisting conditions. However, there may be a waiting period—perhaps a year—for *any* coverage to kick in. And there is no guarantee that your new employer will offer a health care benefit or that coverage—whether sponsored by the employer or bought privately under HIPAA—will be affordable.[7] A separate law (known as COBRA[8]) allows ex-employees of firms with 20 or more workers to continue their old coverage while waiting to sign up with a new employer, but at full cost—without employer subsidy—plus 2 percent. In any event, COBRA does not provide indefinite continuation coverage. Most people are entitled to only 18 months of continuation coverage. You also need to check specifically whether the employer plan offers retirement health benefits to supplement Medicare past the COBRA period or whether benefits are available at all past the COBRA period in case of disability retirement. Even if those benefits are offered at the time you join the firm, the employer may change its mind in the future to cut costs. Thus, you also need to know to what extent you will be *contractually entitled* to those benefits in order to know what the risk of future employer reductions in coverage would be.

You also need to make sure that the insurance company has a good financial strength rating from at least three of the five insurance-rating companies and no so-so ratings. A.M. Best, Standard & Poor's, and Weiss Research have a rating for almost every insurer. Additional ratings are available from Moody's or Fitch. In general, A.M. Best is considered the best marker.

Overall ratings can be obtained on the internet (see resources at the end of the book); the ratings can also be obtained in the special ratings issue of "The Insurance Forum," P.O. Box 245-J, Ellettsville, IN 47429. This publication shows each insurer's rating from these rating companies except A.M. Best. It also explains the meaning of each rating. You can also call the rating services directly. (See phone numbers and websites listed in "Resources" at the end of this book.) A summary of the ratings systems' highest ratings can be found in Appendix 5. When looking for a sound insurance company, you want an A or

[6] It is for that reason that I advise most people not to rely on employer-sponsored plans. See discussion below.

[7] See footnote 1.

[8] The Consolidated Omnibus Budget Reconciliation Act of 1985 was an obscure federal budget bill. However, attached to it was a very important provision for insurance consumers who obtained coverage through employer sponsorship. According to this provision, if you quit your job or have your hours reduced, of if you are fired (unless the reason is gross misconduct), your employer must offer you and your dependents continued coverage.

A+ from A.M. Best and AAA from at least one of the other major rating firms—Moody's, Standard & Poor's Corp. (S & P), Fitch and Weiss.

HMOs are not rated by these agencies. Nevertheless, one way to sniff out a potential failure in an HMO that contracts with independent doctors and hospitals is to get the past three annual lists of its providers. If a lot of them are dropping out, that's a bad sign. With Multiple Employer Welfare Arrangements (MEWAs), which sign up small companies that cannot afford coverage from the major insurers, the sign of a high-risk plan is lower monthly premiums than the competition offers. You should also avoid new MEWAs.

5. It Matters When You Were Born

Traditionally, financial planners have assumed that retirement age is 65, in conjunction with the Social Security retirement age requirements. As a consequence, many insurance products have policy provisions tied to that age. For example, term life insurance coverage may cease or be reduced at age 65. Long-term disability insurance benefits may cease at age 65, and eligibility for disability benefits also may cease at age 65. Many health insurance plans stop paying benefits at age 65. These policies are tied to the assumption that Social Security retirement and Medicare benefits become available at age 65.

These assumptions are not necessarily correct. The age for collecting full Social Security benefits will be increased from age 65 to 67 on a phased-in basis, beginning for those born after 1937.[9] The retirement age will become 67 for those born after 1959. Consequently, it is critical to determine whether your insurance plan incorporates insurance products that cease or reduce coverage or benefits before your actual minimum full benefit Social Security retirement age. If this is the case, and you do not take remedial action, you may discover that you will have gaps in coverage between age 65 and the age you actually become eligible for full Social Security and Medicare benefits.

6. What Really Matters Is Keeping Your Own Cash

Most people think of health care coverage as coming in one blanket insurance policy. They seek that one all-inclusive item in the marketplace, and if they cannot get what they are looking for because of a preexisting condition, they assume that they are essentially being denied the opportunity to do adequate protection planning for their own health risks. Good insurance planning requires different thinking. *As long as you have the money available for your needs when they occur, it does not really matter where it comes from.*

An insurance policy is nothing more than a contract. You, the consumer, agree to pay an insurer a particular amount of money in exchange for which the insurer agrees to compensate you for particular expenses you incur in connection with certain health casualties. In that sense, health insurance can be thought of as a form of casualty insurance. Like other forms of casualty insurance, you need to pay special attention to the types of casualties that are addressed, under what circumstances payment will occur, and what exactly the insurer has agreed to pay when the casualty occurs.

[9] Appendix 4 contains a table summarizing the new retirement age rules.

The purpose of health insurance is to protect you and your family against the potentially catastrophic costs of medical expenses that can accompany a serious illness. Thus, in the overall scheme of things, health insurance is simply a means of protecting your other assets from the financial *risks* that can accompany a serious illness.

You should also think of money as something I refer to as a "fungible" commodity. Fungible simply means that one dollar is the same as the next. There is nothing unique about a dollar bill that is any different from any other dollar bill. Of course, taking into account tax and investment strategies, not all dollars are necessarily equal. But for our purposes, we are going to think about dollars in a straight-on fashion. One is just about as good as the next—as long as they are both controlled by you. Note that I deliberately did not use the word *owned* here. You do not have to *own* a dollar to make use of it. Instead, you may have control of it, for example, by virtue of a contract. As long as you have a "controllable" dollar, you are in the driver's seat and can make *use* of that dollar as you deem necessary.[10]

Because one dollar is as good as the next, it really is of no consequence *where* a dollar comes from as long as it is controllable for use in a particular way. For example, if you know that you will be in the hospital and have bills as a result, it does not matter whether you have traditional hospitalization to cover those expenses as long as you know you have other controllable dollars coming from somewhere other than out of your own pocket to pay those bills.

If you break down the traditional *risks* covered by major medical and hospitalization under those circumstances, you will discover that you are actually dealing with five separate general elements of risk. These include (1) major medical for any preexisting health condition; (2) major medical for all other health conditions; (3) hospitalization for any preexisting health condition; (4) hospitalization for all other health conditions; and (5) adequate provisions for home or long-term health services. If you can devise a combination package of controllable dollars from various sources to ameliorate each of these risks independently, you do not need to find one blanket traditional health insurance policy to achieve the same protection. The goal is simply to match the specific risk with an instrument or collection of instruments that will adequately compensate for that risk.

7. Your Premium Is Not Your Whole Cost of Protection

"Cost" is the difference between what you pay and what you get back. The total cost of insurance protection should be evaluated in terms of all of the realistic risks being protected against and the benefits obtained, not just by the title of the insurance product being purchased or the amount of the premium. This is a difficult concept for many people to grasp. For example, the cost of health insurance cannot be evaluated by the cost of the premium alone. Instead, the cost of ameliorating the *risk* should be evaluated. That may include costs of not only deductibles and copayments but also the entire cost of noncovered items

[10] It is quite possible, for example, to take some commercial insurance products marketed to vitiate one form of risk and instead apply them to another form of risk entirely. In some instances, commercial insurance products may legitimately be used as mechanisms for wealth accumulation, in addition to or instead of simply to address issues of risk. For example, see the discussion about hospital indemnity insurance.

(including those items that become noncovered because the policy becomes exhausted).[11] If, for example, you have no coverage for durable medical equipment and you need a wheelchair, your cost is not simply the premium, deductibles, and copayments; it will also include the *entire cost of the wheelchair.* The same is true of the "stop-loss" or catastrophic limitation included in a health insurance policy. Anything that exceeds that limitation which is not covered by the policy must be added to the "stop-loss" benefit stated in the policy to determine what the catastrophic limit really is.

The concept is similar for life insurance. If you pay a premium for life insurance and get nothing back, your cost for the death protection is the premium. If you pay a premium and get something back later on, such as a cash value, your cost is smaller than the premium. In order to compare the cost of policies, you need to look at premiums, cash values, and dividends (if you have a participating policy).

[11] This issue of exhausting the policy can get very tricky if a single policy has a low maximum policy benefit, was taken out years ago (and has not kept up with inflation), or covers a large family group with a single maximum policy benefit. Under any of these circumstances, it is more likely that the policy by its own terms will not cover all expenses incurred, and this must be taken into consideration to determine the real cost versus benefits of the policy.

EXERCISE 1
Catalog Your Present Insurance Coverage

Your first task in the process of planning is to get organized. To help you gather together your insurance information in a logical system, you should consider establishing a sort of insurance coverage filing system. To follow my suggested system, you will need to gather the following supplies:

- Several good three-ring binders (at least three).
- One small notebook.
- One three-hole punch.
- A box of top-loading sheet protectors (you can obtain these at an office supply store).
- A box of white gummed labels.
- Several sets of notebook index dividers that you can write on.
- As many worksheets as are necessary for each type of policy (one page per insurance policy), including one page for each type of employer-provided insurance benefit from each employer. These worksheets can be found immediately following this section. The "index identification" fields on the worksheets will be created during this exercise.[12]

The first order of business is to organize your policies. Each policy with all its relevant notices, copies of premium paid stubs, annual summaries, and so forth, should be filed *together* in one top-loading sheet protector. You should use one gummed label on the outside of each sheet protector to identify the type of policy, who is covered, the annual premium amount, and the insurance company. You should use another gummed label to assign an index identification number (discussed later). If you do not have an actual policy but only an employee handbook, you need to treat each type of employer benefit as a separate insurance policy by copying the relevant portions of the employee handbook for each insurance type (life, health, disability, other), placing each in its own sheet protector and labeling them accordingly. If you have nothing in writing and you have employment-based insurance coverage, you need to make a point to obtain a written summary of your employer plan. Most employees are entitled to this under the provisions of a federal law known as ERISA.

---

[12] If you have Medicare, Medigap, or both, you should put your Medicare information in one sheet protector along with the Medicare worksheet, and your Medigap policy along with Medigap information in a separate sheet protector. For the Medigap plan, you should also complete a worksheet for the appropriate type of health plan.

After you have obtained, loaded, and labeled all the relevant insurance information, it is time to index it. You should group similar policies together by type (life, health, disability, other) and subtype (e.g., whole life, universal life, term life, endowed, variable). Note that your employer plans will be broken up by type, not stored as a group. Load the notebooks with a single type of insurance in each, even if the binder is not full; if the binder is overfilled, store the insurance type in more than one binder. You should used a gummed label to mark the spine of the binder to indicate the type of insurance policies in the binder. You then need to prepare the index dividers to separate the policies by subtypes. After you have loaded, marked, and placed indexes in the binders, you can create an overall index. You should use the second gummed label on the sheet protectors to mark the policy by type (L for life, D for disability, H for health, O for other), by subtype (e.g., W for whole), and finally by number. For example, my large New York Life whole life policy is listed as L-W-1. This makes each policy easy to identify and find. You should create a master index for each binder and an overall master index. In addition to helping in the planning process, the indexes will help you determine when a policy is missing or out of order.

After your index identification for each policy is created, it is time to start taking an assessment of the content of each of the policies in summary, standardized format so that you may begin to evaluate your coverage and your potential coverage gaps. Each policy should have one worksheet filled out about it. You should also complete one worksheet for each benefit to which you are entitled, even if it does not take the form of an actual insurance policy. For example, if you have an open worker's compensation claim and would be entitled to a death benefit if you died while the claim is open, you should fill out a worksheet for that death benefit as if it were a life insurance policy. Additionally, you should fill out a worksheet for your open worker's compensation claim as if it were a disability insurance policy. This also applies to state disability benefits. Finally, you should fill out a worksheet for any medical benefits to which you are entitled as part of that open claim as if it were a traditional health insurance policy.

Much of the information you will need can be taken from the policies themselves. Other information, such as the insurer's financial strength rating, will have to be located elsewhere. Some of the information (e.g., annual premiums, net cash values, net benefits) will have to be calculated based on other information contained in the policies or on statements that should be stored with the policy in the same sheet protector. If the policies use *formulas,* you should note the formulas and the current amount the formula would yield. For example, if an amount is based on annual income, you should note "annual income" on the worksheet and what the actual annual income is.

After all the necessary worksheets have been completed, they should be punched and placed in the small binder in index order. An overall master policy index should be created and placed at the front of the small binder. At the end of this exercise, you will create a spreadsheet that will assist you in the following sections of this workbook.

Although this exercise involves only the types of insurance that are directly affected by the diagnosis of a chronic illness, you may extend the system to include other insurance coverage, such as homeowner's, automobile, title, commercial, and umbrella liability policies. For these types of insurance, you may want to start separate binders for auto, home, personal, and business.[13]

The following instructions will guide you in completing the worksheets for your policies. The order of discussion is life insurance, disability insurance, health insurance, and long-term care insurance (stored in binder marked "other").

Life Insurance Policy Worksheet Instructions[14]

Index ID is the identifier you assigned to the policy in the earlier exercise.

Annual Premium is the total amount you pay for the policy in a year. If you make monthly payments, multiply your monthly premium by 12; if quarterly, multiply by 4. Do not include items such as interest or principal payments on policy loans. *Waiver of Premium* refers to a policy provision that will continue the insurance in force without the payment of premium during any qualified period of disability (as defined by the policy).

Insurer's Financial Strength Rating must be obtained by either telephone or the Internet. Use the instructions contained on pages 5–6. You may use any of the raters listed there, but make sure that you obtain the rating for the actual company that underwrites your policy.

Contact information for the insurance company should be located on the policy. If not, call your agent and obtain it for your own records. If a group policy, note which group sponsored the plan on the worksheet.

Contact information for your agent should be stored with your policy. If not, write it down and store it with your policy. If you have no agent, leave this blank.

Policy Number is the number the insurance company uses to identify your specific policy. This may sometimes be referred to as the "certificate number" or some other name.

Name of Insured is the person who must die for the insurance policy to pay off. It is not the person who will receive the money (this person is called the "beneficiary").

Birthdate of Insured is the birthdate of the insured listed above. This is important because most term life insurance policies reduce or cease coverage at some point, usually age 65.

Name of Owner is the person who has the right to determine, for example, who the beneficiary will be. This is usually the person who is responsible for paying the premium.

---

[13] The best treatment of general, non-health based insurance planning written for general consumers is *Making the Most of Your Money* by Jane Bryant Quinn (see the reference in "Additional Resources" at the end of the book).

[14] An example of a completed worksheet for a life insurance policy—cross-referenced to the policy, is included at the end of these instructions.

Name of Beneficiary is the person who will receive the proceeds when the policy pays off. If more than one, note all beneficiaries and portions.

Type of Policy is determined by what the annual premium pays for. For example, if there is no investment component to the policy, it is pure term; if the insurance pays a sum or income to you, it is endowment insurance; if the policy develops cash values over time and does not automatically discontinue at a particular age, it is whole life. The type of policy is usually identified at the beginning of the policy.

Date Issued is the date on which the insurance coverage first became effective.

If term, quote from the policy the provision that states how and when the insurance coverage will decrease, if any. Additionally, calculate the amount of insurance that will be available to the insured at ages: 50, 55, 60, 65, 70, 75, and note that on the worksheet.

If term, quote from the policy the provision that states when the insurance coverage will cease. If based on the insured's age, calculate that on the worksheet.

Face Amount refers to the basic amount that the policy promised to pay upon death when you purchased it.

Additional Death Benefits refer to any additions to the death benefits that the policy provides by its terms, such as paid-up additions. If such benefits are available, note them on the worksheet (including any formulas necessary to determine such benefits).

Loans Outstanding as of Today refers to loans against an endowment or whole life policy cash value that you have taken (not available for term life policies). These loans reduce the amount that will be paid to the beneficiary upon death and usually require annual interest payments calculated as provided for in the policy.

Total Cash Value As of Today refers to the amount that you would get from the company if you cashed in your endowment or whole life policy today (usually based on a formula, such as total cash value minus outstanding loans). Term life policies do not accrue cash values.

Living Benefits Provision refers to any part of the policy that expressly allows the beneficiary or insured to obtain at least a portion of the proceeds of the policy before the insured dies, as long as the insured is terminally ill. These benefits are available to assist the insured with expenses at the end of life while they are still alive. If such a provision exists, quote it on the worksheet.

Income Provision refers to the sum or income the insurance company will pay you if you live to a certain age.

Life Insurance Policy Worksheet

Today's Date and Policy Index ID: ______________________________

Annual Premium (amount)/Waiver of Premium (yes/no): ________________

Insurer's Financial Strength Rating: ______________________________

Name, Address, and Phone Number of Insurance Company/Agent/

Group Affiliation: ______________________________________

____

Policy Number: ______________________________________

Name of Insured: ______________________________________

Birthdate of Insured: ___________________________________

Name of Owner: ______________________________________

Name of Beneficiary: ___________________________________

Type of Policy (term, whole, universal): __________________________

Date Issued: ____

If term, formula for decrease of coverage (based on insured's age): _______

____

If term, date coverage ceases (based on insured's age): ______________

____

Face Amount of Policy: _________________________________

Additional Death Benefits as of Today: ___________________________

Loans Outstanding as of Today: _______________________________

Total Cash Value as of Today: ________________________________

Living Benefits Provision, if any: _______________________________

____

Income Provisions (if endowment): ______________________________

____

Term Life Insurance Policy Worksheet Example

Life Insurance Policy Worksheet

Today's Date & Policy Index ID:

Annual Premium (amount)/Waiver of Premium (yes/no) (no waiver provision in policy)

Insurer's Financial Strength Rating:

Name, Address and Phone Number of Insurance Company/Agent:

Policy Number:

Name of Insured:

Birthdate of Insured: 1/1/1955

Name of Owner:

Name of Beneficiary:

Type of Policy (term, whole, universal): Term

From Schedule of Insurance—see item (D) p. 16 → **Date Issued:** 6/1/94

If term, formula for decrease of coverage (based on insured's age): See Schedule of Insurance p. 16

From Schedule of Insurance—see item (C) p. 16 → **If term, date coverage ceases (based on insured's age):** Age 80 = 3/14/2035

From Schedule of Insurance—see item (B) p. 16 → **Face Amount of Policy:** $90,000.00 decreasing with age

Additional Death Benefits as of Today: N/A

Loans Outstanding as of Today: N/A

Total Cash Value as of Today: N/A

From Accelerated Death Benefit Rider—see item (A) p. 17 → **Living Benefits Provision, if any:** 25% Accelerated Death Benefit; See Rider

Income Provisions (if endowment): N/A

Under Age 65	$90,000
Age 65–69	45,000
Age 70–74	22,500
Age 75–79	11,250

Term Life Insurance Policy Imaged Example

GROUP INSURANCE CERTIFICATE ("Certificate")

POLICYHOLDER:

POLICY NUMBER:

certifies that you become an Insured Person on the Insurance Date stated on the Data Page if you: (a) pay the Contribution; and (b) are alive when the Contribution is paid and are alive on the Insurance Date. However, if on the Insurance Date stated on the Data Page, you are: (1) confined at home; (2) confined in a hospital or other medical institution; or (3) incapacitated so as to be unable to perform your normal activities; the Insurance Date is the day you are no longer so confined or so incapacitated, if: (1) such day is within three months of the date insurance would otherwise have taken effect; and (2) you are still an Eligible Person on that day.

The Dependent Insurance section of the Important Notice provisions gives details for Eligible Dependents.

Insurance is subject to: (a) the terms and conditions of the Policy; (b) underwriting requirements; and (c) the Maximum Benefit sections.

Highlights and other details of insurance appear on the Data Page, in the Schedule and in the State Regulations provisions. The Data Page, the Schedule and the applicable State Regulations provisions are attached to and made a part of this Certificate.

This Certificate replaces all Certificates and Certificate Riders, if any, previously issued to an Insured Person under the Policy.

<u>Right To Examine The Certificate For 30 Days</u>.

An Insured Person will have 30 days to examine his or her Certificate. If the Insured Person does not wish to keep the Certificate, it must be surrendered to New York Life within this period. Upon such surrender, will return any premium paid and insurance will be void from the start.

Secretary President

GMR-C-FP 9/1/91

Term Life Insurance Policy Imaged Example (*continued*)

GROUP INSURANCE CERTIFICATE

GROUP INSURANCE CERTIFICATE DATA PAGE

SCHEDULE OF INSURANCE

INSURED PERSON	INSURANCE DATE	AGE AT DEATH	LIFE OPTION
MEMBER	(D) 06/01/94	UNDER AGE 65	$ 90,000.00 (B)
		AGE 65 THRU 69	$ 45,000.00
		AGE 70 THRU 74	$ 22,500.00
		AGE 75 THRU 79 (C)	$ 11,250.00

THIS DATA PAGE IS PART OF YOUR CERTIFICATE OF INSURANCE AND REPLACES AND SUPERCEDES ANY OTHER DATA PAGE PREVIOUSLY ISSUED.

Term Life Insurance Policy Imaged Example (*continued*)

GROUP INSURANCE CERTIFICATE RIDER
to be attached to and made a part of the Certificate

agrees that the Certificate is changed as follows:

As of the later of the Effective Date or the Coverage Date of your Certificate, the following Accelerated Death Benefit is added to the Certificate:

ACCELERATED DEATH BENEFIT

will pay a benefit for a Covered Person's Terminal Illness in accordance with all of the following.

Definitions **Terminal Illness** means a medical condition where the patient has a life expectancy of 12 months or less.

For The Benefit To Be Paid For the benefit to be paid the Insured Person must give:

1. the Policyholder a completed, written request for the benefit on a form satisfactory to and
2. satisfactory proof that the Covered Person has a Terminal Illness. (A)

What Benefit Is Payable The benefit payable is 25% of the amount of insurance in force on the Covered Person's life on the date approves the Insured Person's request for the Accelerated Death Benefit.

The benefit will be paid in a lump sum and is payable once while the Covered Person is insured under the Policy, whether insurance is continuous or interrupted. Any benefit payable for a Covered Person's loss of life will be reduced by the amount paid on his or her behalf under the Accelerated Death Benefit.

Who Will Be Paid Any benefit payable will be paid to the Insured Person, except that: If has received satisfactory proof of the Insured Person's death before such payment is made, payment will be made in accordance with the applicable beneficiary provisions.

When Insurance Ends Insurance in force on a Covered Person's life will end on the earlier of: (a) the day before the day the amount of such insurance less the amount paid on his or her behalf under the Accelerated Death Benefit equals zero or less; or (b) the date insurance would otherwise end as stated on the When Insurance Ends page(s), except that: An Insured Person may choose to continue his or her Dependent Life Insurance, if his or her insurance ended because the amount of such insurance less the amount paid on his or her behalf under the Accelerated Death Benefit equals zero or less.

Secretary President

Term Life Insurance Policy Imaged Example (*continued*)

TABLE OF CONTENTS

IMPORTANT NOTICE

Certificate This Certificate is a summary of the provisions of the Policy. It should be kept in a safe place. It is not a contract of insurance. Any conflict between the terms of the Certificate and the Policy will be decided in favor of the Policy. A copy of the Policy is available at the Endowment's office for inspection at any time during business hours. The Insured Person should contact the Endowment or with questions regarding insurance.

Errors Errors, or delays in keeping records will: (a) not revoke insurance otherwise in force; (b) not continue insurance which otherwise would have ended; and (c) upon discovery, require fair adjustment of premium and/or insurance to correct the error.

Policy The Policy is a contract between the Endowment . In accordance with the provisions of the Policy, and without the consent of Covered Persons, the Policy may be changed and/or the Policy may be terminated. The complete terms and conditions governing insurance are in the Policy.

Incontestability Except as stated below, cannot contest the validity of: (a) an Insured Person's insurance or his or her Dependent Insurance after it has been in force for two years; (b) an Insured Person's insurance or his or her Dependent Insurance after it has been in force for two years after restoration; and/or (c) the amount of an increase in insurance on a Covered Person after such increase in insurance has been in force for two years; under the Policy, during such Covered Person's lifetime.

If the validity of insurance in force on a Covered Person is contested, will only rely upon written statements signed by the Insured Person and/or his or her Insured Dependent in applying under the Policy for: (a) insurance; (b) restoration of insurance; or (c) an increase in insurance, but only for the amount of such increase. However, a copy of that statement must be furnished to such person or to his or her beneficiary. Such statements are representations, not warranties.

Exceptions: may, at any time, contest the validity of insurance in force on a Covered Person, if such contest is: (a) based upon provisions which relate to eligibility for insurance; or (b) for non-payment of Contributions.

Examination at its own expense, has the right and opportunity to in the event of loss of life: (a) request an autopsy where it is not forbidden by law or religious belief; and/or (b) examine the medical records of the deceased; to determine the cause of the loss.

Term Life Insurance Policy Imaged Example (*continued*)

IMPORTANT NOTICE (Continued)

Dependent Insurance An Insured Person can elect to become insured for Dependent Insurance for each of his or her Eligible Dependents by requesting such insurance and giving satisfactory evidence of insurability, as required.

Except as stated below, such Dependent Insurance will take effect on the applicable date stated on the Data Page if the Insured Person: (a) pays the Contribution;
(b) and such dependent are both alive when the Contribution is paid and are both alive on the Insurance Date; and (c) is an Insured Person on the Insurance Date.

Exceptions

1. Except as stated in 3. below, if the Insured Person has Dependent Insurance in force for children, any child he or she later acquires or requests to insure will become insured on the day such child becomes an Eligible Child.

2. If determines that any proof of good health is not satisfactory with respect to any Eligible Dependent, Dependent Insurance for each Eligible Dependent for whom satisfactory evidence of insurability was given will take effect as described above if, in addition, the Insured Person authorizes , in writing, to exclude from Dependent Insurance any Eligible Dependent whose proof is not satisfactory. The Insured Person can later reapply for Dependent Insurance for any Eligible Dependent so excluded.

3. If, on the date Dependent Insurance would otherwise have taken effect, such Eligible Dependent is:

   a. confined at home;
   b. confined in a hospital or other medical institution; or
   c. incapacitated so as to be unable to perform his or her normal activities;

   the Insurance Date for such Eligible Dependent is the day such Eligible Dependent is no longer so confined or so incapacitated, if:

   a. such day is within three months of the date insurance would otherwise have taken effect;
   b. the person who applied for such Dependent Insurance is an Insured Person on that day; and
   c. such dependent is still an Eligible Dependent on that day.

Term Life Insurance Policy Imaged Example (*continued*)

LIFE INSURANCE

will pay a benefit for an Insured Person's loss of life in accordance with all of the following:

For The Benefit To Be Paid For the benefit to be paid, must receive satisfactory proof of the Insured Person's loss of life no later than two years after the date of such loss or as soon as reasonably possible after that.

What Benefit Is Payable Except as stated below, the benefit payable is the applicable Amount Of Life Insurance under the Life Option in force for the Insured Person on the date of his or her loss of life, subject to the Maximum Benefit section. A single payment is made unless payment in installments has been requested in accordance with the Payment In Installments section.

Exception

If an Insured Person's death: (a) is due to or related to: (1) suicide; (2) an attempt at suicide; or (3) an intentionally self-inflicted injury; (b) occurs during an attempt at suicide; or (c) occurs while intentionally injuring himself or herself;

whether such Insured Person was sane or insane at the time of such death and such death was within two years after: (a) the initial Insurance Date of any Life Option for which he or she was insured; or (b) the Insurance Date of any Life Option which resulted in an increase in the Insured Person's Amount Of Life Insurance, but only for the amount of such increase; only liability will be for a return of the applicable premiums paid to

Maximum Benefit The maximum benefit under the Policy for an Insured Person's loss of life is the applicable Amount Of Life Insurance under the highest Life Option under the Policy. Unless agreed to by the Endowment and , an Insured Person can be insured for only one Life Option at any one time.

If an Insured Person is insured for an Amount Of Life Insurance which exceeds the maximum benefit, it will be reduced to the maximum benefit as of the date such maximum was exceeded by reducing or terminating insurance as necessary. Any insurance so reduced or terminated will be considered null and void and the premium will be equitably adjusted.

Aggregate Maximum If the Insured Person is insured under the Policy or the Policy the sum of his or her life insurance will not exceed the maximum benefit. If such sum exceeds the maximum benefit, it will be reduced to the maximum benefit as of the date such maximum was exceeded by reducing or terminating insurance as necessary. Any insurance so reduced or terminated will be considered null and void and the premium will be equitably adjusted.

Who Will Be Paid Except as stated below, the benefit will be paid as follows:

a. If only one beneficiary is named and survives the Insured Person, payment will be made to such beneficiary.

b. If more than one beneficiary is named and they are not classified as Primary Beneficiary and/or Contingent Beneficiary, payment of the stated shares will be made to each surviving named beneficiary.

c. If more than one beneficiary is named and they are classified as Primary Beneficiary and/or Contingent Beneficiary, payment will be made to the surviving Primary Beneficiaries as stated by the Insured Person. Unless otherwise stated by the Insured Person, if more than one Primary Beneficiary is named and shares are stated for each and: (1) only one Primary Beneficiary survives the Insured Person, he or she will receive the share of any Primary Beneficiary who does not survive the Insured Person; or (2) more than one Primary Beneficiary survives the Insured Person, the surviving Primary Beneficiaries will share equally the share of any Primary Beneficiary who does not survive the Insured Person.

Term Life Insurance Policy Imaged Example (*continued*)

LIFE INSURANCE (Continued)

d. If no Primary Beneficiaries survive the Insured Person, payment will be made to the surviving Contingent Beneficiaries as stated by the Insured Person.

Unless otherwise stated by the Insured Person, if more than one Contingent Beneficiary is named and shares are stated for each and: (1) only one Contingent Beneficiary survives the Insured Person, he or she will receive the share of any Contingent Beneficiary who does not survive the Insured Person; or (2) more than one Contingent Beneficiary survives the Insured Person, the surviving Contingent Beneficiaries will share equally the share of any Contingent Beneficiary who does not survive the Insured Person.

e. If more than one beneficiary is named and the Insured Person has not stated the shares and they are: (1) not classified as Primary Beneficiary and/or Contingent Beneficiary, the surviving named beneficiaries will share equally; and (2) classified as Primary Beneficiary and/or Contingent Beneficiary, the surviving Primary Beneficiaries will share equally. If no Primary Beneficiaries survive the Insured Person, the surviving Contingent Beneficiaries will share equally.

f. If is unable to pay all or part of the benefit, as stated by the Insured Person in accordance with any of the above, or if the Insured Person fails to name a beneficiary, payment will be made as follows: (1) to his or her surviving spouse; (2) if his or her spouse does not survive, equally to his or her surviving children, or to the survivor; (3) if no children survive, equally to his or her surviving parents, or to the survivor; (4) if neither parent survives, equally to his or her surviving brothers and sisters, or to the survivor; or (5) if no brothers or sisters survive, to the executors or administrators of his or her estate.

<u>Exceptions</u>

a. Subject to the Facility Of Payment Exception and unless otherwise stated by the Insured Person, the benefit will be paid to the Insured Person's beneficiary last recorded under an individual policy, if:

   (1) application for the individual policy was made under a conversion right;
   (2) the benefit is not payable under the individual policy;
   (3) the individual policy, if issued, is surrendered to and
   (4) the benefit is paid under the Policy.

b. **Common Disaster** – Subject to the Facility Of Payment Exception, if any beneficiary dies at the same time as or within 30 days after the Insured Person suffers a loss of life, but before has received satisfactory proof of such loss, payment will be made as though that beneficiary had died before the Insured Person suffered such loss.

c. **Facility Of Payment** has the right to pay up to $2,000 of the benefit to anyone who has incurred expenses for the Insured Person's fatal illness or the Insured Person's burial ("payee").

   If a beneficiary or a payee is a minor or is, in opinion, not legally able to give a valid receipt for any payment due him or her, payment may be made in monthly installments of up to $50 each to any person or institution who, in opinion, is caring for or supporting such beneficiary or payee. These monthly installments will continue until the earlier of the date:

   (1) claim is made by a duly appointed guardian, committee of the beneficiary or payee for the remainder of the benefit, if any; or
   (2) all of the benefit, to which such beneficiary or payee is entitled, has been paid.

   Such payment will be proper to the extent made.

Term Life Insurance Policy Imaged Example (*continued*)

LIFE INSURANCE (Continued)

Naming/Changing A Beneficiary To name a beneficiary or change a beneficiary designation, the Insured Person must give a completed, written request on a form satisfactory to Such request must be: (a) approved by and (b) recorded by or on behalf of

After such recording, the designation will take effect as of the date the request was signed, subject to any payment made or other action taken by or on behalf of before such recording.

One or more beneficiaries can be named. If more than one beneficiary is named, they can be classified as Primary Beneficiary and/or Contingent Beneficiary. The Insured Person can state each beneficiary's share.

Payment In Installments The Insured Person can elect to have all or part of the benefit paid in installments. He or she can later revoke or change such election.

After the Insured Person's death, his or her beneficiary can elect to have all or part of the benefit, to which he or she is entitled, paid in installments, if: (a) the Insured Person did not elect payment in installments; (b) the beneficiary is a natural person; and (c) no payment has been made.

The beneficiary can later revoke or change his or her election.

For each election or change, must be given a completed, written request on a form satisfactory to . Such request must be: (a) approved by ; and (b) recorded by or on behalf of .

After such recording, the election or change will take effect as of the date the request was signed, subject to any payment made or other action taken by or on behalf of before such recording.

The amount and terms of the installments will be in accordance with standard practices at the time of such election or change.

Transfer Of Ownership To transfer all incidents of ownership of an Insured Person's Life Insurance, the Insured Person must give a completed, written request on a form satisfactory to Such request must be: (a) approved by ; and (b) recorded by or on behalf of

After such recording, the transfer will take effect as of the date the request was signed, subject to any payment made or any action taken by or on behalf of before the recording.

The Endowment agrees to accept the Contribution directly from the transferee.

Except as stated above, an Insured Person's insurance under the Policy cannot be transferred or assigned.

Term Life Insurance Policy Imaged Example (*continued*)

WHEN INSURANCE ENDS

When An Insured Person's Insurance Ends Without prejudice to an existing claim and except as stated in the applicable Continuance provisions, an Insured Person's insurance will end on the earliest of:

1. midnight of the last day of the Insurance Period during which the Insured Person is no longer a full-privileged voting member of the Endowment;

2. midnight of the last day of the Insurance Period for which the last Contribution has been paid;

3. the Insured Person's Termination Age Date;

4. midnight of the day before the date the Policy is changed to end insurance for the group of insureds to which the Insured Person belongs; or

5. midnight of the day before the date the Policy terminates, or midnight of a later date agreed upon by the Endowment and .

When An Insured Person's Dependent Insurance Ends Without prejudice to an existing claim and except as stated in the applicable Continuance provisions, an Insured Person's Dependent Insurance for each of his or her Insured Dependents will end on the earliest of:

1. the time the Insured Person's insurance ends;

2. with respect to the insurance for an Insured Spouse:

   (a) midnight of the last day of the Insurance Period during which the Insured Person's marriage ends by divorce or annulment;

   (b) midnight of the last day of the Insurance Period for which the last Contribution has been paid for such spouse; or

   (c) the Survivor Dependent spouse's Termination Age Date;

3. with respect to the insurance for an Insured Child:

   (a) midnight of the last day of the Insurance Period during which such Insured Child marries;

   (b) midnight of the last day of the Insurance Period during which such Insured Child does not meet the support requirement;

   (c) such Insured Child's Termination Age Date; or

   (d) midnight of the last day of the Insurance Period for which the last Contribution has been paid for the Dependent Child Unit;

4. midnight of the day before the day such Insured Dependent becomes an Insured Person; or

5. midnight of the day before the day the Policy is changed to end insurance for the group of insureds to which the Insured Dependent belongs.

Term Life Insurance Policy Imaged Example (*continued*)

CONTINUANCE - LIFE INSURANCE ("CONTINUANCE")

An Insured Person's Life Insurance will continue, after the date it would otherwise have ended as stated in the When Insurance Ends provisions, in accordance with the following:

Conversion Period Benefit The maximum amount of Life Insurance the Insured Person is eligible to convert will: (a) continue during the Conversion Period; and (b) be payable, if he or she suffers a loss of life during the Conversion Period.

Grace Period Benefit A grace period of 31 days is granted for the payment of each Contribution other than the first Contribution. Insurance in force will continue, but not beyond the date it would otherwise end as described in the When Insurance Ends provisions. The benefit for the Insured Person's loss of life will be paid if such loss occurs within the grace period, if the Contribution is paid. The amount of such insurance is subject to any applicable reductions at the specified Ages stated on the Data Page.

CONTINUANCE - DEPENDENT LIFE INSURANCE ("CONTINUANCE")

An Insured Person's Dependent Life Insurance for each of his or her Insured Dependents will continue, after the date it would otherwise have ended as stated in the When Insurance Ends provisions, in accordance with the following:

Conversion Period Benefit The maximum amount of Dependent Life Insurance the Insured Dependent is eligible to convert will:

a. continue during the Conversion Period; and
b. be payable, if he or she suffers a loss of life during the Conversion Period.

Grace Period Benefit A grace period of 31 days is granted for the payment of each Contribution other than the first Contribution. Insurance in force will continue, but not beyond the date insurance would otherwise end as described in the When Insurance Ends provisions. The benefit for the Insured Dependent's loss of life will be paid if such loss occurs within the grace period, if the Contribution is paid. The amount of such insurance is subject to any applicable changes at the specified Ages stated on the Data Page.

Survivor Dependent Spouse Benefit Insurance in force on the day the Insured Person dies will continue if: (a) the Insured Person's Insured Spouse survives him or her; (b) the applicable conversion right on the death of the Insured Person has not been exercised, as stated in the Conversion Rights provisions; and (c) the Contribution has been paid.

The amount of such insurance is subject to any applicable reductions at the specified Ages stated on the Data Page. However, the Contribution for the Spouse Option will be based on the Survivor Dependent spouse's Age.

This benefit will end on the earlier of: (a) the date insurance would otherwise end as described in the When Insurance Ends provisions; or (b) midnight of the last day of the Insurance Period during which the Survivor Dependent spouse: (1) remarries; or (2) dies.

Term Life Insurance Policy Imaged Example (*continued*)

DEFINITIONS

"Age" means: (a) on any June 1, the attained age on such June 1; or (b) on any other date, the attained age on the immediately preceding June 1.

"Contingent Beneficiary" (Second Beneficiary) means the person or persons named to receive the proceeds of insurance under the Policy, upon the death of the Insured Person, if no Primary Beneficiary survives the Insured Person.

"Contribution" means the applicable full periodic contribution toward the premium, received by the Endowment, which one of the following persons must pay for insurance to take effect on the Insurance Date and/or for insurance to continue in force under the Policy: an Insured Person; a Survivor Dependent; or any other person as required by the Endowment. "Contribution" is due on each Contribution Date and is determined by the Endowment.

"Contribution Date" means the following dates on which the Contribution must be paid to the Endowment:

a. for the first Contribution: (1) on or before the Insurance Date; or (2) if by agreement between the Endowment and and without individual selection, no later than 31 days after the Insurance Date; and
   The first Contribution will be reduced pro rata if the Insurance Period from the first Contribution Date to the next Contribution Date is less than: (1) 12 months if the mode of payment is annual; (2) 6 months if the mode of payment is semiannual; and (3) 3 months if the mode of payment is quarterly.
b. for each later Contribution: (1) each June 1 for the annual mode of payment; (2) each June 1 and December 1 for the semiannual mode of payment; (3) each June 1, September 1, December 1 and March 1 for the quarterly mode of payment;

"Conversion Period" means the 31 day period, immediately after the date insurance would otherwise end, during which a Covered Person can exercise a conversion right.

"Covered Person" means an Insured Person or an Insured Dependent.

"Dependent Child Unit" means, on any given day, all the Insured Dependents of each Insured Person.

"Dependent Insurance" means an Insured Person's insurance with respect to his or her Insured Dependent(s).

"Eligible Dependent" means a person who is one of the following:

a. an Eligible Person's or an Insured Person's spouse identified on the request for group insurance form, if such spouse is a resident and/or citizen of the United States or Canada, except a person residing in an Excluded State; or
b. an Eligible Person's or an Insured Person's unmarried child, who: (1) is at least 6 months of age; (2) has not exceeded the Maximum Eligibility Age; and (3) is a resident and/or citizen of the United States or Canada, except a person residing in an Excluded State.

Child means a natural child, a stepchild, an adopted child or a foster child, who must be dependent upon the Eligible Person or the Insured Person for support.

If both parents of an Eligible Child are Insured Persons, such child will be considered an Eligible Dependent of only one parent.

"Eligible Dependent" does not include a person who is an Eligible Person or Insured Person.

References to **"Eligible Spouse"** and **"Eligible Child(ren)"** mean the same as "Eligible Dependent spouse" and "Eligible Dependent child(ren)", respectively.

"Eligible Person" means a person who: (a) is a full-privileged voting member of the Endowment; (b) has not exceeded the Maximum Eligibility Age; and (c) is a resident and/or a citizen of the United States or Canada, except a person residing in an Excluded State.

Term Life Insurance Policy Imaged Example (*continued*)

DEFINITIONS (Continued)

"Excluded State" means: for a person whose residence and principal place of business or normal activity are in the

"Insurance Date" means the applicable date that:

a. insurance takes effect for: (1) an Eligible Person; and/or (2) each Eligible Dependent of an Insured Person; and/or

b. a change in insurance takes effect for: (1) an Insured Person; and/or (2) each Insured Dependent of an Insured Person.

"Insurance Period" means the span of time from an Insured Person's Contribution Date through the day before his or her next Contribution Date, during which an Insured Person's insurance and/or Dependent Insurance continues, if the Contribution for such span of time is paid; except that:

If the Insured Person does not remit the full Contribution covering the span of time from one Contribution Date through the day before his or her next Contribution Date, such span of time will be reduced to the period starting from the Insured Person's Contribution Date through the date for which such partial Contribution can continue such insurance and/or Dependent Insurance in force.

"Insured Dependent" means one of the following persons who is insured under the Policy, as approved by an Eligible Dependent; or a Survivor Dependent.

References to **"Insured Spouse"** and **"Insured Child(ren)"** mean the same as "Insured Dependent spouse" and "Insured Dependent child(ren)", respectively.

"Insured Person" means an Eligible Person who is insured under the Policy, as approved by

"Maximum Eligibility Age" means the oldest a person can be and still be initially eligible for insurance, as follows:

Eligible Person And Eligible Dependent	Age
Eligible Person	through age 69
Eligible Child	through age 24

"Primary Beneficiary" (First Beneficiary) means the person or persons named to first receive the proceeds of insurance under the Policy upon the death of the Insured Person.

"Survivor Dependent" means an Insured Dependent of a deceased Insured Person.

"Termination Age Date" means the date insurance for a Covered Person ends due to attainment of a specific age, as follows:

Midnight of the May 31st which immediately follows the:

a. Insured Person's 80th birthday;
b. Survivor Dependent spouse's 80th birthday; or
c. Insured Child's 25th birthday;

except that: If such birthday is May 31st, insurance will end at midnight of that day.

Term Life Insurance Policy Imaged Example (*continued*)

SCHEDULE

Change In Option – Increase An Insured Person, who is less than Age 70, can increase his or her Amount Of Life Insurance and/or Amount Of Dependent Life Insurance by replacing an existing Life Option and/or Spouse Option with another Option which is available to him or her, if the person to whom the increase applies is not a resident of an Excluded State. The new Option will take effect in accordance with the following:

For The New Option To Take Effect – For the new Option to take effect, the Insured Person:

a. must give the Endowment a completed, written request for the new Option on a form satisfactory to as required;
b. must give satisfactory evidence of insurability;
c. must pay the Contribution;
d. must be alive when the Contribution is paid and must be alive on the Insurance Date, if he or she is requesting an increase in the Amount Of Life Insurance; and
e. and the Insured Dependent to whom the increase applies must both be alive when the Contribution is paid and must both be alive on the Insurance Date, if the Insured Person is requesting an increase in the Amount Of Dependent Life Insurance.

When The New Option Takes Effect – The new Option takes effect on the Insurance Date. Except as stated below, the Insurance Date is the first day of the calendar month after the date (a) establishes that its underwriting requirements are met; and (b) approves such new Option.

Exceptions

a. If such date is the first day of the calendar month, the Insurance Date is that day.

b. If on the date the new Option would otherwise have taken effect, the Covered Person to whom the increase applies is: (1) confined at home; (2) confined in a hospital or other medical institution; or (3) incapacitated so as to be unable to perform his or her normal activities;

   the Insurance Date is the day he or she is no longer so confined or so incapacitated, subject to the following:

   (1) if the request is for an increase in an Insured Person's Amount Of Life Insurance: (a) the Insured Person must still be both an Insured Person and an Eligible Person on that day; and (b) such day must be within three months of the date insurance would otherwise have taken effect; and
   (2) if the request is for an increase in an Insured Person's Amount Of Dependent Life Insurance: (a) the Insured Person must still be an Insured Person on that day; (b) such day must be within three months of the date insurance would otherwise have taken effect; and (c) the Insured Dependent to whom the increase applies must still be both an Insured Dependent and an Eligible Dependent on that day.

Change In Option – Decrease An Insured Person can decrease his or her Amount Of Life Insurance and/or Amount Of Dependent Life Insurance by replacing an existing Life Option and/or Spouse Option with another Option which is available to him or her. The new Option will take effect in accordance with the following:

For The New Option To Take Effect – For the new Option to take effect, the Insured Person must: (a) give the Endowment a completed, written request for the new Option on a form satisfactory to as required; and (b) pay the Contribution;

When The New Option Takes Effect – The new Option takes effect on the Insurance Date. Except as stated below, the Insurance Date is the first day of the calendar month after the date (a) establishes that its underwriting requirements are met; and (b) approves such new Option.

Exception If such date is the first day of the calendar month, the Insurance Date is that day.

Disability Insurance Policy Worksheet Instructions

Even though there is no specific space for it, you need to note the contact information for the company, and if applicable, the agent for each insurance policy as well as any group affiliation (if the policy is based on group membership). Contact information for the insurance company should be located on the policy. If not, call your agent and obtain it for your own records. Contact information for your agent should be stored with your policy. If not, write it down and store it with your policy.

Insurer's Financial Strength Rating must be obtained by either telephone or the Internet. Use the instructions contained on pages 5–6. You may use any of the raters listed there, but make sure you obtain the rating for the actual company that underwrites your policy.

Annual Premium is the total amount you pay for the policy in a year. If you make monthly payments, multiply your monthly premium by 12; if quarterly, multiply by 4. *Waiver of Premium* refers to a policy provision that will continue the insurance in force without the payment of premium during any qualified period of disability (as defined by the policy).

Policy Number is the number the insurance company uses to identify your specific policy. This may sometimes be referred to as the "certificate number" or some other name.

Name of Insured is the person who must become disabled within the meaning of the policy for the insurance policy to pay off. *Birthdate of Insured* is the birthdate of that person. This is important because most disability insurance policies cease coverage at some point—usually age 65 if based on age.

Term of Policy means the maximum length of time that the disability benefits will be paid. Most policies pay either for a specified number of months or years or until a particular age is reached.

Noncancellable and guaranteed renewable: Examine your policy to see if you have the right to renew your policy despite claims made, and circle yes/no on the worksheet; also see if you have protection against cancellation by the insurance company despite claims made, andcircle yes/no on the worksheet (which, by the way, also protects against premium increases based on claims).

Monthly Benefits refers to the gross number of dollars you would receive from the policy each month if you were disabled today within the meaning of the policy, without regard to any offsets stated in the policy. If this number is based on a formula or a reference number (e.g., your salary), note both the number and the formula from which it was derived.

Any Offset Amounts refers to whether there are any negative adjustments such as offsets if you are receiving other benefits (e.g., Social Security, other disability insurance, worker's compensation, etc.). If your policy has offset provisions, list the type of offset and any formula to compute the offset (e.g., if the offset is dollar-for-dollar, specify it as equal to benefit). Also calculate the actual amount of any offers in dollars if claims were made today.

Cost-of-Living Adjustments, if any, refers to provisions that increase your monthly benefits after you are disabled based on increases in the cost-of-living due to inflation. If this is tied to an index, state the index.

Who Pays Premium: This determines taxation of policy proceeds. If you pay the premium out of your own pocket the policy proceeds are nontaxable. If your employer pays, then all proceeds are taxable as ordinary income.

Net Benefit/Percentage of Current Monthly Income: This provision requires a calculation. You must first determine your monthly income using your household budget. Then calculate the ratio of the net monthly disability benefit (after offsets) to your own monthly income. For example, if you typically receive monthly income of $5,000 after taxes and your disability income net benefit (after taxes) is $2,500, per month, it represents 50% of your monthly income.

First: monthly income from family budget ______________________

Second: net monthly disability benefits (after offsets) ______________

Third: compute any taxation on net benefits and subtract from net benefits

Fourth: compute ratio: [amount under "first"] / [amount under "third"]

____

(express in terms of percentage). You may also wish to compute the number of dollars short of 100% with all policies combined to know what your budget shortfall may be if you became disabled today.

Elimination Period: The amount of time that must elapse between the beginning of the disability and when payments will begin under the policy.

Date Coverage Ceases (if based on insurer's age): If your insurance policy pays until a particular age (e.g., 65), calculate the date on which coverage ceases based on the insured's current age. You may want to compare this with your social security eligibility date (see Appendix 4).

Event Upon Which Coverage Ceases (if based on insured's group affiliation or employment): If your insurance policy only covers you while you are employed or a member of some organization, note that limitation. Also, if your employment must be full-time or a minimum number of hours per week, note this fact along with how the plan defines eligibility.

Initial Definition of Disability: Cite the specific language the policy uses to define when an insured will be considered disabled. Inability to perform your own job? Inability to perform any job? Does the policy cover both accidents *and* illnesses?

Further Definition of Disability: If the definition of disability changes after a period of time (e.g, after 2 years of disability), note the new specific language the policy uses to define when an insured will be considered eligible for continued disability after that time.

Partial Disability or Rehabilitation Coverage: Note the language of any partial disability or rehabilitation coverage provisions in your policy. Also, make a note if these benefits are absent, in which case only a total disability is compensable. If your disability merely limits the types or amounts of work you are able to perform—even if your pay is decreased—you may not be able to make up any part of the shortfall without this type of coverage.

Index Identification is the identifier you assigned to the policy in the earlier exercise.

Further Options: Does the policy offer options to buy additional coverage at a later time, without evidence of medical insurability? If so, note that fact, and *when* the option dates occur.

Disability Insurance Policy Worksheet

Today's Date: ____________________

Annual Premium (amount)/Waiver of Premium (yes/no): ____________________

____

Name, Address, Phone Number, and Financial Strength Rating of Insurance Company: ____________________

Name, Address, and Phone Number of Agent or Group: ____________________

Policy Number: ____________________

Name and Birthdate of Insured: ____________________

Term of Policy (maximum benefit period): ____________________

Noncancellable or guaranteed renewable? (Yes/No)
(If yes, circle which one) ____________________

Monthly Benefit (amount or formula): ____________________

Any offset amounts: ____________________

Cost-of-Living Adjustments, if any: ____________________

Who Pays Premium (circle one) self/employer/other: ____________________

Net Benefit/Percentage of Current Monthly Income: ____________________

Elimination Period: ____________________

Date Coverage Ceases (if based on insured's age): ____________________

Event Upon Which Coverage Ceases (if based on insured's affiliation or employment): ____________________

Initial Definition of Disability: ____________________

Further Definition of Disability (after elapsed period): ____________________

____

Partial Disability or Rehabilitation Coverage: ____________________

____

Index Identification: ____________________

____

Further Options: ____________________

Disability Insurance Policy Imaged Example

Disability Insurance Policy Worksheet

Today's Date:

From Schedule of Insurance—see item (A) p. 34

Annual Premium (amount)/Waiver of Premium (yes/no): $529.90

From page 39, Waiver of premium benefit, item (B) Totally disabled for at least 90 consecutive days

Name, Address, Phone Number, and Financial Strength Rating of Insurance Company:

Name, Address and Phone Number of Agent:

Policy Number:

Name and Birthdate of Insured:

From Schedule of Insurance item (C) p. 34 See also p. 41, item J.

Term of Policy (maximum benefit period): 65–75 depending on age of onset

Noncancelable or guaranteed renewable? (Yes/No) (If yes, circle which one) (D) From Face Sheet

From Schedule p. 35, item (E)

Monthly benefit amount or formula: $1,000 plus COLA

Any offset amounts: None stated

Item (F) from Schedule p. 35 and Rider, p. 45

Cost-of-Living Adjustments, if any: Yes Max 6%→Tied to Consumer Price Index (see Rider, p. 45)

Net Benefit/Percentage of Current Monthly Income:

Item (G) from schedule, p. 34

Elimination Period: 2 months

Item (C) from schedule, p. 34

Date coverage ceases (if based on insured's age): 60–75 depending on age of onset

Event upon which coverage ceases (if based on insured's affiliation or employment): N/A Coverage is portable

Item (H) Quote from p. 37

Initial Definition of Disability: "Your Occupation"

Further Definition of Disability (after elapsed period): N/A

Item (I) from Residual disability benefit provision, p. 44

Partial Disability or Rehabilitation Coverage: 20%–30% income loss coverage

Index Identification of Policy:

Disability Insurance Policy Imaged Example (*continued*)

Noncancellable and guaranteed renewable to age 65
Conditionally renewable after age 65 – Premiums can change

hereby furnishes insurance to the extent set out in this policy. All of the provisions on this and the pages which follow are part of this policy.

Secretary President

You means the person insured. **We** or means Insurance Company

D

Noncancellable and guaranteed renewable to age 65

You may renew this policy at the end of each term until you are age 65. During that time, we cannot change the premium or cancel this policy.

Conditional right to renew after age 65 — Premiums can change

After you are age 65, you may renew this policy at the end of each term as long as you are at work full time. There is no age limit. But you must be at work at least thirty hours each week for at least ten months each year.

Your premium will be at our rates then in effect for persons of your age and class of risk. We have the right to change such premiums on a class basis on any policy anniversary.

Notice of ten day right to review policy

You have ten days to review this policy from the date you receive it. Within that time, you can deliver or mail it to our home office or to any Guardian agent or agency for a prompt refund of all premiums. This policy will then be void from the start.

Professional Disability Income Policy

Participating

Disability Insurance Policy Imaged Example (*continued*)

S C H E D U L E P A G E

INSURED-

OWNER-

LOSS PAYEE-

POLICY NUMBER-

DATE OF ISSUE-

TERM- 3 MONTHS

PREMIUM DISCOUNT CLASS- NONSMOKER

ANNUAL PREMIUM FOR:

- BASIC BENEFITS - $355.90.
- RESIDUAL INDEMNITY RIDER - $72.10.
- COST OF LIVING ADJUSTMENT RIDER - $101.90.

TOTAL ANNUAL PREMIUM - $529.90.
TERM PREMIUM - $139.18. (A)

AS A MEMBER OF A SPONSORING ASSOCIATION, YOUR PREMIUMS SHOWN HERE WILL BE REDUCED BY 10 PER CENT ON EACH PREMIUM DUE DATE.

--- ELIMINATION PERIOD --- (G)

2 MONTHS

--- BENEFIT PERIOD --- (C)

TO AGE 65 IF DISABILITY BEGINS BEFORE AGE 60
60 MONTHS IF DISABILITY BEGINS AT OR AFTER AGE 60 BUT BEFORE AGE 61
48 MONTHS IF DISABILITY BEGINS AT OR AFTER AGE 61 BUT BEFORE AGE 62
42 MONTHS IF DISABILITY BEGINS AT OR AFTER AGE 62 BUT BEFORE AGE 63
36 MONTHS IF DISABILITY BEGINS AT OR AFTER AGE 63 BUT BEFORE AGE 64
30 MONTHS IF DISABILITY BEGINS AT OR AFTER AGE 64 BUT BEFORE AGE 65
24 MONTHS IF DISABILITY BEGINS AT OR AFTER AGE 65 BUT BEFORE AGE 75
12 MONTHS IF DISABILITY BEGINS AT OR AFTER AGE 75

SCHEDULE PAGE 1

CONTINUED......

Disability Insurance Policy Imaged Example (*continued*)

POLICY NUMBER – G-507817

--- TABLE OF BASIC BENEFITS ---

– MONTHLY INDEMNITY	$1,000. (E)
– MAXIMUM REHABILITATION BENEFIT	$12,000.
– CAPITAL SUM	$12,000.

--- TABLE OF OPTIONAL BENEFITS ---

THE RENEWAL PROVISION OF EACH OPTIONAL RIDER MAY DIFFER FROM THAT OF THIS POLICY. SEE EACH RIDER FOR DETAILS.

– RESIDUAL DISABILITY

–COST OF LIVING ADJUSTMENT

MAXIMUM INCREASE PER CENT – 06 PER CENT (F)

--- BENEFITS AND PREMIUMS AFTER AGE 65 ---

IF YOU RENEW THIS POLICY WHEN YOU ARE AGE 65, WE WILL ISSUE A NEW SCHEDULE PAGE AT THAT TIME. BENEFITS WILL BE LIMITED TO THOSE SHOWN IN THE TABLE OF BASIC BENEFITS ABOVE.

PREMIUMS FOR THIS POLICY MAY INCREASE ON RENEWAL AT OR AFTER AGE 65 AND WILL BE AT OUR RATES THEN IN EFFECT FOR PERSONS OF YOUR AGE AND CLASS OF RISK.

SCHEDULE PAGE 2

Disability Insurance Policy Imaged Example (*continued*)

Page two

This policy is a legal contract between you and . READ IT WITH CARE.

INDEX

The major provisions of this policy appear on the following pages:

Additional benefits, if any, are shown in the schedule page and are described in the rider forms attached to this policy.

SCHEDULE PAGE

Disability Insurance Policy Imaged Example (*continued*)

Exclusions and limitations

Preexisting condition limitation

We will not cover loss that begins in the first two years after the date of issue from a preexisting condition.

A *preexisting condition* means a physical or mental condition:

- which was misrepresented or not disclosed in your application; and
- for which you received a physician's advice or treatment within two years before the date of issue; or
- which caused symptoms within one year before the date of issue for which a prudent person would usually seek medical advice or treatment.

Medical care requirement

We will not pay benefits under this policy for any period of disability during which you are not under the care of a physician.

We will waive the medical care requirement during any claim under this policy upon reasonable proof that your sickness or injury no longer requires regular care of a physician under prevailing medical standards. Such waiver will not restrict our rights under the provision of this policy called "Physical examinations."

Definitions

Benefit period

The benefit period is shown in the schedule page. It is the longest period of time for which we will pay indemnity for continuous disability from the same cause.

Elimination period

The elimination period is shown in the schedule page. It is a consecutive number of days for which we will not pay benefits at the start of a claim. You must be disabled on all of those days.

Injury

Injury means accidental bodily injury which occurs while this policy is in force.

Loss payee

You are the loss payee unless some other person is named in the schedule page. We will pay all benefits to the loss payee.

Monthly indemnity

The monthly indemnity is shown in the schedule page. It is the amount we will pay for each month of total disability.

Owner

You are the owner unless some other person is named in the schedule page. The owner has the right to renew this policy; to request a change in benefits; to change the loss payee; to receive dividends, if any are declared; and to vote for our directors.

Physician

Physician means a legally qualified physician other than yourself, who is not a loss payee or owner under this policy.

Sickness

Sickness means a sickness or disease, including a pregnancy, which is first diagnosed and treated while this policy is in force.

Total disability (H)

Total disability means that, because of sickness or injury, you are not able to perform the major duties of your occupation.

Occupation means your regular occupation or profession at the time you become disabled.

If you have limited your professional practice to a recognized specialty in medicine, dentistry, law, or accounting, we will deem your specialty to be your occupation.

You will be totally disabled even if you are at work in some other capacity so long as you are not able to work in your occupation.

Disability Insurance Policy Imaged Example (*continued*)

Page four

Benefit provisions

Total disability benefit

When you are totally disabled, we will pay the monthly indemnity as follows:

- You must become totally disabled while this policy is in force.
- You must remain so disabled to the end of the elimination period. No indemnity is payable during that period.
- After that, monthly indemnity will be payable at the end of each month while you are totally disabled.
- Monthly indemnity will stop at the end of the benefit period or, if earlier, on the date you are no longer totally disabled.

We will not increase the rate of monthly indemnity because you are totally disabled from more than one cause at the same time.

Fractional month

We will pay benefits at the rate of 1/30 of the monthly indemnity for each day for which we are liable when you are disabled for less than a full month.

Interrupted elimination period

We will allow a break in the elimination period if you make a brief recovery before it ends. But the break may not last longer than six months or, if less, the length of the elimination period.

Then if you are again disabled from the same or a different cause, we will combine the two periods of disability to determine when benefits begin.

Waiver of elimination period

We will waive the elimination period if you become disabled within five years after the end of a prior period of disability which lasted more than six months and for which we paid benefits.

Recurrent periods of disability

We will consider recurrent periods of disability from the same cause or causes to be one continuous period of disability unless each period is separated by a recovery of six months or more.

Capital sum benefit

The capital sum is shown in the schedule page. This lump sum is in addition to any other indemnity payable under this policy.

If you suffer a capital loss and survive it for 30 days, we will pay the capital sum for each such loss. But we will not pay for more than two such losses in your lifetime.

Capital loss

A capital loss means the entire loss of the sight in one eye, with no possible recovery; or the complete loss of a hand or foot by severance through or above the wrist or ankle.

Such loss must occur while this policy is in force and must result from sickness or injury.

If this policy has terminated, we will pay for a capital loss which results from an injury sustained while this policy was in force and which occurs within 90 days after the date of that injury.

Disability Insurance Policy Imaged Example (*continued*)

Presumptive total disability benefit

We will always consider you to be totally disabled, even if you are at work, if sickness or injury results in your loss of:

- the sight of both eyes; or
- the hearing of both ears; or
- the power of speech; or
- the use of any two limbs.

We will waive any unexpired part of the elimination period from the date of loss. We will pay the monthly indemnity each month while such loss continues from the date of loss to the end of the benefit period.

You must give us satisfactory proof of loss. But you do not have to be under the continuing care of a physician.

Rehabilitation benefit

If you enroll in a rehabilitation program while you are totally disabled, we will pay a benefit to meet some of the costs you may incur. All of the following conditions apply:

- We must agree to the program in writing before you enroll.
- The program must be a formal plan of retraining that will help you return to work in your occupation.
- It must be directed by an organization or individual who is licensed or accredited to provide vocational training or education to persons who are totally disabled.
- We will pay only those costs which are not otherwise covered by health care insurance, workers' compensation, or any public fund or program. But we will not pay more than the maximum rehabilitation benefit shown in the schedule page.

Transplant benefit

If you are totally disabled because of the transplant of a part of your body to another person, we will deem you to be disabled as the result of sickness.

Waiver of premium benefit

→ B

If you are totally disabled for at least 90 consecutive days, we will refund any premiums paid during those 90 days. Then we will waive any later premium that falls due while you are continuously so disabled or within 90 days after you recover.

On each waiver, we will renew this policy for another term of the same length as that in effect when claim began. If that term was less than twelve months and you are still disabled and eligible for waiver on a policy anniversary, we will then change the term to twelve months.

You have the right to resume payment of premiums when you recover and the waiver of premium benefit ends. At that time, you can change the term back to its original length if you wish.

Nothing in this provision will change the conditions for renewal after age 65 that require you to be at work full time.

Disability Insurance Policy Imaged Example (*continued*)

Page six

Claim provisions

Notice of claim

You must give us notice of claim within 30 days after any loss which is covered by this policy occurs or starts, or as soon after that as is reasonably possible. Notice, with sufficient information to identify you, will be deemed notice to us if given to us at our home office, or to an authorized agent.

Claim forms

When we get your notice of claim, we will send claim forms for filing proof of loss. If we do not send you such forms within 15 days after your notice, you may submit a written statement, within the time fixed in this policy for filing proof of loss, which proves the nature and extent of the loss for which claim is made.

Time for filing proof of loss

We are liable for benefits at the end of each month while you are disabled beyond the elimination period until the benefit period ends or, if earlier, the date you recover.

You must give us proof of loss at our home office or at any agency office:

- for loss from disability within 90 days after the end of the period for which we are liable; and
- for any other loss within 90 days after the date of loss.

If you cannot reasonably give us proof within such time, we will not deny or reduce claim if you give us proof as soon as possible. But we will not pay benefits in any case if proof is delayed for more than a year, unless you have lacked legal capacity.

Time of payment of claims

Subject to due written proof of loss, we will pay all accrued indemnity for disability each month. Any amounts unpaid when our liability ends will be paid immediately after we receive due written proof of loss.

We will pay benefits for any other covered loss immediately after we receive due written proof of loss.

Payment of claims

We will pay all benefits of this policy to the loss payee.

If you are the loss payee, any accrued benefits unpaid at your death will be paid to your estate.

If any benefit of this policy becomes payable to your estate or to a minor or incompetent person, we may pay such benefit, up to $1,000, to any of your relatives by blood or marriage who we believe has a right to it. Any payment made in good faith under this provision will fully discharge to the extent of such payment.

Physical examination

We shall have the right and opportunity to have you medically examined at our expense when and as often as we may reasonably require while you claim to be disabled under this policy.

Legal actions

No one can bring an action at law or in equity under this policy until 60 days after written proof has been furnished as required by this policy. In no case can an action be brought against more than three years after written proof must be furnished.

Misstatement of age

If your age has been misstated, the benefits will be what the premium paid would have bought at the correct age. If we would not have issued this policy at your correct age, there will be no insurance and we will owe only a refund of all premiums paid for the period not covered by this policy.

Disability Insurance Policy Imaged Example (*continued*)

Provisions relating to premium and renewal

Age

When we refer to a specific age—such as to age 65—we mean your age as of the policy anniversary that first occurs on or after the birthday on which you attain that age.

Policy anniversary

A policy anniversary is the recurrence each year of the date of issue.

Premium and grace period

The term premium is shown in the schedule page. Premiums are due on the first day of each term. You have a grace period of 31 days in which to pay each premium due after the first one.

This policy will stay in force during the grace period. If you have not paid the premium by the end of the grace period, this policy will lapse at 12:01 AM the next day.

If you die, we will refund to your estate that part of any premium which applies to the period after your date of death.

Termination of this policy at or after age 65

(J)

If you are not at work full time at the end of any term when you are age 65 or older, except by reason of total disability, this policy will terminate.

Termination will not prejudice any claim for total disability:

- which begins while this policy is in force; or
- which begins within 31 days after the date of termination as the result of an accident that occurred while this policy is in force.

If we accept any premium after you are age 65, this policy will stay in force to the end of the term which that premium covers.

Reinstatement

If this policy has lapsed at the end of the grace period, you can still keep it in force by paying the first overdue premium within 45 days of the time it was due.

After that, you can reinstate this policy under the following conditions:

- You must complete an application.
- You must pay all overdue premiums, for which we will issue a conditional receipt.
- We will place this policy back in force on the date we approve your application. But if we have not approved or refused your application in writing within 45 days after we have given a receipt, this policy will be reinstated on that 45th day. If we refuse to place this policy back in force, we will refund your premium.

In any case, this policy will be reinstated on the date that we or our agent accept a premium and do not ask for an application.

The reinstated policy will cover only loss that begins after the date of reinstatement. In all other respects, you and we will have the same rights under this policy as before it lapsed, subject to any provisions endorsed on or attached to it in connection with reinstatement.

Suspension during military service

We will suspend this policy on the date you go on active duty in the military service of any country or international authority. Such duty will not include temporary active duty by reservists for military training that lasts 90 days or less. We will refund that part of any premium paid for the period of such suspension.

If your active duty does not last longer than five years, you can place this policy back in force without evidence of good health or earned income as of the date of your discharge. To do so, you must apply in writing and pay the premium, both within 90 days after active duty ends.

We will base your premium on your age and class of risk when this policy was first issued. If you were disabled on or before your date of discharge, you must have recovered for at least six months before we will cover a later disability from the same cause.

Term changes

On any premium due date, you can change the term to twelve months or six months or three months. But we will not allow any change which would result in a premium not being due on a policy anniversary.

Disability Insurance Policy Imaged Example (*continued*)

Page eight

General contract provisions

Consideration

We have issued this policy in consideration of the representations in your application and payment of the first term premium. A copy of your application is attached and is a part of this policy.

Effective date of insurance

Insurance takes effect on the date of issue for the term shown in the schedule page. Each term of this policy starts and ends at 12:01 AM standard time in the place where you live.

Preliminary term: If the schedule page shows a preliminary term and premium, this policy will be in force from the start of that period to the date of issue. All of your rights under this policy will begin on the first day of that term instead of on the date of issue. But this will not change the policy anniversary.

Entire contract; changes

This policy, with its riders and attached papers, if any, is the entire contract of insurance. No change in this policy will be valid unless it has been endorsed on or attached to this policy in writing by the president, a vice president, or the secretary of .

No agent has authority to change this policy or to waive any of its provisions.

Incontestable

(a) After this policy has been in force for two years during your lifetime, we cannot use any misstatements in your application to void this policy or to deny a claim for disability that starts after the end of those two years.

(b) We cannot reduce or deny a claim for any disability that starts after two years from the date of issue on the grounds that a sickness or physical condition had existed before the date of issue, unless we have excluded it by name or specific description before the date of loss.

Conformity with state laws

Any provision of this policy which, on the date of issue, is in conflict with the laws of the state in which you reside on such date is hereby amended to conform to the minimum requirements of such laws.

Provisions relating to mutual insurance

Participation

This policy will be entitled to participate in the divisible surplus of Dividends will be paid in such manner, under such conditions, and to such extent as our board of directors may from time to time determine.

Election of directors

The annual election of directors is held at our home office on the second Wednesday in December. Owners of policies may vote for directors according to the insurance law of the State of For details, write to the

Disability Insurance Policy Imaged Example (*continued*)

Residual disability rider

This rider is part of this policy and subject to all its conditions. It provides indemnity when you are at work at reduced earnings as a result of sickness or injury.

Under the terms of this rider, we will determine whether you are residually disabled solely on the basis of your ability to earn income after you become sick or injured. We will compute benefits solely in relation to earned income that you receive on a cash basis.

Premium and renewal The premium for this rider is shown in the schedule page. You may not renew this rider after you are age 65.

Amendments to this policy

Elimination period The elimination period will begin on the date you become sick or injured. You may be totally or residually disabled on each day after that to satisfy the elimination period under the benefit provisions of this policy or rider.

Waiver of premium You may be totally or residually disabled to meet the conditions for waiver of premium of this policy.

Definitions

Residual disability Residual disability means that you are at work and are not totally disabled under the terms of this policy; but, because of sickness or injury, you are not able to earn at a rate of at least 80% of your prior income.

Residual indemnity The residual indemnity is a reduced amount of the monthly indemnity for this policy. We derive it as follows:

$$\text{residual indemnity} = \frac{\text{loss of income}}{\text{prior income}} \times \text{monthly indemnity}$$

If you have a social insurance substitute rider, we will add the SIS benefit to the monthly indemnity in this equation in each month when the SIS benefit is payable.

Income Income means your gross earned income, less business expenses, but before any other deductions. It includes salaries, wages, fees, commissions, bonuses, business profits or other payments for your personal services. It does not include unearned income from savings, investments, or real property.

Prior income means your average monthly income for the tax year with the highest earnings in the three years just prior to the date on which you became disabled.

Current income means all income which you receive on a cash basis in each month while you are residually disabled.

Loss of income means the difference between your prior income and your current income.

Expenses Expenses mean the regular business expenses which you may deduct from gross earned income for federal tax purposes.

Prior expenses mean your average monthly expenses for the same tax year on which your prior income is based.

Current expenses mean your expenses in each month while you are residually disabled.

During a claim under this rider, the current expenses you deduct from gross earned income may not exceed your prior expenses, except as adjusted by this rider.

Adjustment of prior expenses While you are disabled under this rider, we will adjust your prior expenses to reflect any increase in fixed expenses that you then incur under the terms of a lease or other contract which was in effect at the start of claim.

(continued)

Disability Insurance Policy Imaged Example (*continued*)

Adjustment of prior income and expenses due to inflation

At the end of each twelve months in a continuous claim before you are age 65, we will adjust your prior income and prior expenses to reflect changes in the cost of living since the start of claim.

Review date means the recurrence each year of the date on which you were first disabled in the same claim.

CPI-U means the Consumer Price Index for All Urban Consumers, or any later replacement of it, as published by the federal Department of Labor.

Index month means the calendar month that fell ninety days before the date on which you were first disabled in the same claim.

On each review date in the same claim, we will adjust your prior income and prior expenses for use in the next twelve months by the actual percentage change in the CPI-U since the index month. We will make no change that would reduce those amounts below what they were at the start of claim.

Residual disability benefit

When you are residually disabled, we will pay the residual indemnity each month as follows:

- You must become totally or residually disabled before you are age 65 while this policy is in force.
- You must remain so disabled to the end of the elimination period. No indemnity is payable during that period.
- After that, residual indemnity will be payable at the end of each month while you are residually disabled.

Computation of residual disability benefit

For the first six months while you are residually disabled, the exact rate of your current income will apply, except as stated below. After that, we will compute your residual indemnity for each six month period on the average of your current income for the preceding six months. But we may agree to a shorter or longer period of averaging.

During the first six months for which residual disability benefits are payable, we will deem your loss of income to be 50% of prior income or the actual percentage of loss, if greater.

(I)

After the first six months, loss of income will be computed at the actual percentage rate of loss.

However, at all times, if loss of income is more than 80% of prior income, we will deem such loss to be 100%.

Termination of residual indemnity

Residual indemnity will stop when the first of the following events occurs:

- you become totally disabled; or
- your loss of income is less than 20% of prior income or, if lower, the residual indemnity becomes less than $250 a month; or
- the benefit period ends; or
- you become age 65 in any claim which began before age 60.

Proof of oss

We can require any proof which we consider necessary to establish your current and prior incomes. We have the right to examine your financial records, including your federal tax returns, as often as we may reasonably require.

During claim under this rider, we can require that your accounting practices be the same as those which were in effect at the time you first became disabled.

Disability Insurance Policy Imaged Example (*continued*)

Cost of Living Adjustment Rider

This rider is part of this policy and subject to all its conditions

Premium and renewal

The premium for this rider is shown in the schedule page. You may not renew this rider after you are age 65.

Definitions

Review date means the recurrence each year of the date on which you were first disabled in the same claim.

CPI-U means the Consumer Price Index for All Urban Consumers, or any later replacement for it, as published by the federal Department of Labor. That index shows the rate of change in the cost of living in the United States.

Index month means the calendar month that fell ninety days before the date on which you were first disabled in the same claim.

Monthly indemnity means the monthly indemnity of this policy in effect on the date that claim begins. We base all benefits for disability on the monthly indemnity.

Social insurance substitute

If you have a social insurance substitute rider, we will adjust the SIS benefit under the same conditions which apply to the monthly indemnity. But this will not change the conditions for payment of the SIS benefit.

Cost of living adjustments

At the end of each twelve months in a continuous claim before you are age 65, we will adjust your monthly indemnity for the next twelve months to reflect any changes in the cost of living since the start of claim.

On each review date, we will compare the CPI-U for the index month with the CPI-U for the same month in the year then ended. If the CPI-U has gone up or down since the index month, we will adjust the monthly indemnity for the next twelve months by the percentage change in the CPI-U.

Your adjusted indemnity may go up or down from year to year as the CPI-U rises or falls in relation to the index month. But the adjusted indemnity will never be:

- more than the amount we would pay if the CPI-U had risen each year exactly by the maximum increase per cent shown for this rider in the schedule page.
- less than the monthly indemnity.

When adjustments end

We will adjust the monthly indemnity on each review date until the first of the following events occurs:

- you are no longer disabled; or
- the benefit period ends; or
- you become age 65.

We will make no further changes up or down in the monthly indemnity after you are age 65, except as follows. If you are then disabled in a claim which began at or after age 60, we will continue to make adjustments until the benefit period ends or, if earlier, you are no longer disabled.

Disability Insurance Policy Imaged Example (*continued*)

Adjusted indemnity when claim ends

If your claim ends before you are age 65, we will then deem the monthly indemnity of this policy to be the increased amount, if any, created by this rider on the last review date before claim ended.

The increased indemnity will take effect without an extra premium charge on the date claim ended. We will base all benefits on that amount in any later claim which begins after such date before you are age 65.

This provision will apply at the end of each claim in which this rider operates to increase the monthly indemnity until you are age 65.

We will increase the SIS benefit, if any, in the same way. But this will not change any of the conditions of the social insurance substitute rider for benefit payment or renewal.

Monthly indemnity at age 65

At the time you first renew this policy when you are age 65, you may choose one of the following amounts of monthly indemnity for all claims that begin after that date:

- the monthly indemnity shown in the schedule page; or
- the increased indemnity, if any, last created by this rider.

If you are disabled at age 65, you can make this choice at the time you first renew this policy after you recover.

We will base your premium after that on the amount of monthly indemnity you select. You must meet all the conditions in the provision on the first page of this policy for renewal after age 65.

Indemnity Major Medical and Hospitalization Health Insurance Worksheet Instructions

Index Identification is the identifier you assigned to the policy in the earlier exercise.

Effective Date of Insurance: This is the date on which coverage became effective.

Maximum Lifetime Coverage: The maximum number of dollars that your insurance company is required to spend during the life of your policy. Look for a lifetime maximum of at least $1 million. More is better. The more people covered by your policy, the higher this number should be.

Preexisting Condition Limitation (if any): List any exclusion used by insurers to avoid paying for care to treat a medical disease or condition that was or could have been diagnosed before enrollment under the policy. Quote the actual policy language here.

Preexisting Condition Waiting Period (if any): List any period of time that must elapse after policy enrollment before the insurer will pay for care to treat a medical disease or condition that was or could have been diagnosed before enrollment, as defined by the policy.

Date of Expiration of Waiting Period: Calculate—Effective date of insurance, moved forward for the waiting period, if any.

Annual Premium: The total amount you pay for the policy in a year. If you make monthly payments, multiply your monthly premium by 12; if quarterly, multiply by 4.

Insurance Contact Information: Name, address, phone number of insurance company.

Insurer's Financial Strength Rating must be obtained by either telephone or the Internet. Use the instructions contained on pages 5-6. You may use any of the raters listed there, but make sure you obtain the rating for the actual company that underwrites your policy.

Insurance Agent or Group Contact Information: Name, address, and phone number of agent or any group sponsor.

Policy or Identification Numbers: The number used by the company to identify your particular insurance contract.

Identity and Birthdate(s) of Insured(s): Name all persons insured, and list their birthdates.

Noncancellable and guaranteed renewable: Examine your policy to see if you have the right to renew your policy despite claims made, and circle yes/no on the worksheet; also see if you have protection against cancellation by the insurance company despite claims made, and circle yes/no on the worksheet (which, by the way, also protects against premium increases). You want to make sure that your policy is at least guaranteed renewable. This will prevent the insurer from discontinuing your coverage if you become ill (although by itself this will not preclude the insurer from raising rates on an *individual* policy based on claims expenses). For a group policy, rates must be increased for the entire group at once.

Date Coverage Ceases (if based on insured's age, for each insured): If your insurance policy pays until a particular age (e.g., 65), calculate the date on which coverage ceases based on the insured's current age.

Event Upon Which Coverage Ceases (if based on insured's affiliation or employment): If your insurance policy covers you only while you are employed or a member of some organization, note that limitation. Also, if your employment must be full-time or a minimum number of hours per week, note this fact along with how the plan defines eligibility.

Standard Annual Deductible: List the amount the insured must pay before the insurer begins to pay toward the cost of health services otherwise covered under the plan.

Catastrophic (or "Stop-Loss") Out-of-Pocket Expense Limitation: List the maximum covered out-of pocket expenses that the policy requires you to pay before it will cover the rest of your insured expenses.

Any Other Contributions or Copayments: List any other expenses, portions of expenses, or contributions of covered items that your policy requires you to pay.

Lifetime Limit: List the maximum dollar amount that the insurance will pay in total benefits in your lifetime under this policy. Also note whether this limit is for an individual, a specific health condition, or all covered members of a family group.

Health Insurance Policy Worksheet: Indemnity Major Medical and Hospitalization (Part A)

Today's Date and Index ID of Policy: ______________________

____

Effective Date of Insurance and Maximum Coverage Period: __________

Preexisting Condition Limitations: ______________________

If Preexisting Condition Waiting Period, Date of Expiration of Period: ______

____

Annual Premium (12 times monthly or 26 times biweekly): __________

Insurance Contact Information and Insurer Financial Strength Rating: ______

Agent or Group Contact Information (if applicable): __________

Policy or Identification Numbers: ______________________

Identity and Birthdate(s) of Insured(s): ______________________

Is policy noncancellable or guaranteed renewable?:(Yes/No) (If yes, circle which one) ______________________

Date Coverage Ceases (if based on insured's age, for each insured): ______

____

Event Upon Which Coverage Ceases (if based on insured's affiliation or employment): ______________________

____

Standard Annual Deductible: ______________________

Catastrophic (or "Stop-Loss") Out-of-Pocket Expense Limitation: ________

____

Any Other Contributions or Copayments: ______________________

____

Lifetime Limit: ______________________

____

Health Insurance Policy Imaged Example

Health Insurance Policy Worksheet: Indemnity Major Medical & Hospitalization (Part A)

Today's Date & Index ID of Policy:

Effective Date of Insurance and Maximum Lifetime Coverage Period: 3/1/98 From Schedule of Insurance, item (A), p. 52

5 years of age 65. From Schedule of Benefits—item (F), p. 54

Pre-Existing Condition Limitations: See item B, p. 10. Note: This is not a complete exclusion for pre-existing conditions
from page 10

If Pre-Existing Condition Waiting Period, Date of Expiration of Period: maximum = 3/1/2000 (24 months)

Annual Premium (12 times monthly or 26 times biweekly):

Insurance Contact Information & Insurer Financial Strength Rating:

Agent Contact Information (if applicable):

Policy or Identification Numbers:

Identity and Birthdate(s) of Insured(s):

Is policy noncancelable or guaranteed renewable?: (Yes/No) (If yes, circle which one)
Policy is group plan and subject to changes made for group as a whole.

From policy p. 55, item (G)

Date coverage ceases (if based on insured's age, for each insured): No date certain; continued membership in group required; no age limit.

Event upon which coverage ceases (if based on insured's affiliation or employment):

From Schedule of Benefits, item (C), p. 54

Deductible: (Deductible not annual here) $25,000 during 36 consecutive month period

Catastrophic (or "stop-loss") Out-of-Pocket Expense Limitation:
N/A

From Schedule of Benefits, item (D)

Any other Contributions or Co-Payments: None, but policy limited to schedule of benefits maximum

Lifetime Limit:
$2,000,000

Item (E) from p. 54

Health Insurance Policy Imaged Example (*continued*)

CERTIFICATE OF INSURANCE

The term "Data Page" refers to the form which is inserted behind this page.

certifies that the person named on the Data Page is insured for the benefits described in this certificate. This insurance is subject to the eligibility and effective date requirements of the group policy.

NOTE: If you **are insured** for dependents' insurance covering your spouse and/or your child(ren), Spouse's Effective Date and/or Child(ren)'s Effective Date will appear on the Data Page. If you **are not insured** for dependents' insurance, the Data Page will only show Member's effective date.

DATE YOUR INSURANCE TAKES EFFECT

Your insurance will take effect on the date shown on the Data Page. You might be hospitalized on the date your insurance is to take effect. If so, insurance will take effect the day after you are discharged. This requirement will not apply to you if you were insured under the Prior Plan (as defined on page DEF).

CANCELLATION DURING FIRST 30 DAYS

You may cancel the insurance described in this certificate at any time during the 30 day period after you receive this certificate. Mail this certificate with your written request for cancellation to the
will promptly refund the premium paid.

IMPORTANT NOTICE

This certificate is a summary of the group policy provisions which affect **your** insurance. It is merely evidence of the insurance provided by such policy.

The group policy is a contract between and the Policyholder. It may be changed or ended without notice to or consent of any insured person.

This certificate replaces any certificate previously issued by to you under the group policy.

The benefits described in this certificate are provided by group policy
the Policyholder.

The provisions set forth in the group policy are changed to comply with the minimums which may be required by applicable law in the state in which you are a resident.

Health Insurance Policy Imaged Example (*continued*)

GROUP INSURANCE CERTIFICATE

GROUP INSURANCE CERTIFICATE DATA PAGE

POLICYHOLDER:

GROUP POLICY NUMBER: CERTIFICATE HOLDER ID:

SCHEDULE OF INSURANCE

INSURED

DEDUCTIBLE AMOUNT = $ 25,000.00
PLAN OF INSURANCE = PLAN II
CONVALESCENT CARE WEEKLY BENEFIT: $500

MEMBER'S CURRENT EFFECTIVE DATE: 03/01/98 → (A)

INITIAL EFFECTIVE DATE

MEMBER'S INITIAL EFFECTIVE DATE: 12/01/91

THIS DATA PAGE IS PART OF YOUR CERTIFICATE OF INSURANCE AND REPLACES AND SUPERSEDES ANY OTHER DATA PAGE PREVIOUSLY ISSUED.

DATE PREPARED: 02/18/98

Health Insurance Policy Imaged Example (*continued*)

CERTIFICATE INDEX

Each section in this certificate has a 2 line code at the end. The code "G-19001" means that the page belongs to the certificate series. The letter or letters below the certificate code represents a phonetic description of the particular section (FP = Face Page; E = Eligibility). If a section requires more than one page, the descriptive letter is followed by a number indicating its order in the section (D-2 is the second page in the Dependent Eligibility section).

This index refers you to the phonetic codes.

Health Insurance Policy Imaged Example (*continued*)

SCHEDULE OF BENEFITS FOR INJURIES OR SICKNESSES COMMENCING ON OR AFTER MARCH 1, 1994

EXCESS MAJOR MEDICAL BENEFITS FOR ALL INSURED PERSONS

Deductible for each person per injury or sickness	**see Data Page**	C
Deductible accumulation period	36 consecutive months	C
Benefit period, per injury or sickness	the greater of: • 5 years, or • age 65	F
Excess major medical benefits to be paid during each benefit period after the deductible is satisfied	100% of covered charges	D
Maximum benefit for each person		
• for charges while insured	$2,000,000	E
• for charges to treat psychiatric, mental, nervous or emotional disorders while hospitalized, while insured	$25,000	
• for charges to treat alcoholism, or drug addiction	see page MM-4	
• for charges for hospital room and board, per day	the hospital's average charge for a semi-private room	
• for charges for private duty nursing - per hour - while insured	 $30 $60,000	
• for charges for convalescent care - per week - per confinement	 $100 up to 52 weeks	
• for charges for hospice care and home health care	see page MM-3	
• for charges incurred by a donor(s) for transplant surgery, per injury or sickness	$25,000	

SCH

DEFINITIONS

PHYSICIAN means:

- a medical practitioner licensed to provide medical services and perform general surgery,
- a Christian Science practitioner as recognized by the Christian Science Journal, or
- any other practitioner whose services, by law of the state where such services are performed, must be covered by the group policy.

Each such person must be licensed in the state where he performs the service and must act within the scope of that license. He must also be certified and/or registered if required by such state.

HOSPITAL means:

1. A licensed institution which is approved by the Joint Commission on Accreditation of Hospitals. "Hospital" does not mean a place, or part of one, which is used mainly for:

- the aged
- the chronically ill
- convalescents
- drug addicts
- alcoholics
- a rest home
- a nursing home
- custodial, educational or rehabilitory care, or

2. Any other institution whose services, by law of the state where such services are performed, must be covered by the group policy. Each such institution must be licensed and approved, if required, by the appropriate agency of such state.

Health Insurance Policy Imaged Example (*continued*)

DEFINITIONS (Continued)

TOTAL DISABILITY means that solely due to an injury or sickness the insured person cannot perform the normal activities of a person of like age and sex, with like occupation or retired status.

INSURED PERSON means an insured member or insured dependent.

MEDICARE means Parts A and B of the medical care benefits provided by Title XVIII of the Social Security Act of 1965.

BASIC PLAN means a plan which provides benefits or services for, or by reason of, hospital, surgical or medical care or treatment through:

1. group, blanket, or franchise insurance coverage;

2. group, blanket, or franchise pre-paid plans for:

- group hospital service
- group medical service
- group practice
- individual practice, and
- any other such plans for members of a group;

3. any plan provided by:

- labor management trusts
- unions
- employer organizations
- professional organizations, or
- employee benefit organizations; and

4. a government program or statute, including Medicare, *other than a state medical assistance plan that implements Title XIX of the Social Security Act of* 1965.

PRIOR PLAN means the Policyholder's group insurance plan in effect on February 28,

NOTE: If you **are insured** for dependents' insurance covering your spouse and/or your child(ren), Spouse's Effective Date and or Child(ren)'s Effective Date will appear on the Data Page. If you **are not insured** for dependents' insurance, the Data Page will only show Member's effective date.

DEF-2

ELIGIBILITY

DATE INSURANCE ENDS

Your insurance will end at the earliest of:

1. the date the group policy ends;

(G) 2. the end of the period for which the last premium has been paid for you;

3. the March 1 coinciding with or next following the date you cease being a member in good standing with the American Bar Endowment; or

4. the date you enter the Armed Forces on full-time active duty.

CONTINUATION OF INSURANCE WITH PREMIUM PAYMENT

Your insurance may end due to termination of membership. If you have been insured by the group policy for at least 3 months you may continue your excess major medical insurance by continuing to pay the premiums due. Dependents' excess major medical insurance may also be continued.

Insurance may continue until the earliest of:

- the date the person is eligible for Medicare
- the end of a period of 9 months
- the date the person is insured under another group insurance plan, or
- the date the group policy ends.

E(YY)

Health Insurance Policy Imaged Example (*continued*)

EXCESS MAJOR MEDICAL BENEFITS

The provisions set forth in the Excess Major Medical Benefits section of the group policy are changed to comply with the minimums which may be required by applicable law in the state in which you are a resident.

If an insured person incurs the covered charges listed below due to an injury or sickness, United States Life will pay the benefits described below.

Benefits will be paid **only** for the covered charges incurred by an insured person for an injury or sickness which exceed the greater of:

1. the amount payable for the injury or sickness by a basic plan, or
2. the amount of the deductible.

All injuries suffered in one accident will be considered one injury. All sicknesses due to related causes, and complications of such causes will be considered one sickness, unless complete recovery from the one condition occurred before a later condition began.

DEDUCTIBLE

The deductible is the amount of covered expenses that **each insured** must incur for each injury or sickness *before* any benefits are paid by United States Life. These expenses must be for covered charges incurred within a period of time called the deductible accumulation period.

The deductible and the deductible accumulation period are shown in the Schedule of Benefits.

BENEFIT PERIOD

Benefits are payable starting on the date an insured person incurs charges for an injury or sickness in excess of the deductible. The benefit period will begin on the date on which the first covered charge is incurred that is used to satisfy the deductible for such injury or sickness.

Benefits may be paid for such injury or sickness during the period of time called the benefit period. The benefit period is shown in the Schedule of Benefits.

Benefits for any injury or sickness will end on the earlier of:

- the date the applicable maximum benefit has been paid, or
- the end of the benefit period.

A new benefit period cannot be established for the same injury or sickness once the benefit period expires.

if 2 or more insured family members are injured in the same accident

The covered charges incurred by **each** such insured person due to the accident will be combined. If the total exceeds one deductible amount, no further deductible will be required for such insured persons for any injury caused by the accident.

MAXIMUM BENEFIT

The maximum amount of benefits to be paid for all injuries or sicknesses for each person is shown in the Schedule of Benefits.

MM-1-DIS

COVERED CHARGES

The charges covered by this benefit section are those listed below. Any amount of such charges which exceeds reasonable and customary charges will not be covered.

REASONABLE AND CUSTOMARY CHARGE means a charge not more than the usual charge for medical treatment in the locality where it is received. The nature and severity of the injury or sickness involved will be taken into account.

Covered charges are:

1 Charges made by a hospital for:

- room and board, up to the amount shown in the Schedule of Benefits, and
- services and supplies.

D-2(WW) —6— E-160,071

Health Insurance Policy Imaged Example (*continued*)

EXCESS MAJOR MEDICAL BENEFITS (Continued)

COVERED CHARGES (Continued)

2. Charges made by a convalescent home for confinement for convalescent or custodial care, up to the amount shown in the Schedule of Benefits.

The confinement must begin within 14 days after hospitalization ends. Such hospitalization must have lasted for at least 3 days for which room and board benefits are paid. The confinement must be:

- due to the injury or sickness which required the hospitalization, and
- recommended, approved or certified by a physician as necessary and reasonable.

Successive confinements will be considered one confinement unless they are due to unrelated causes.

CONVALESCENT HOME means a licensed institution that has on its premises:

- organized facilities to care for and treat its patients
- a staff of physicians to supervise such care and treatment, and
- a registered nurse on duty at all times.

"Convalescent home" does not mean a place, or part of one, which is used mainly for:

- the aged
- alcoholics
- drug addicts
- persons with mental, nervous or emotional disorders.

3. Charges made by a physician for:

- diagnosis
- treatment, and
- surgery.

4. Charges made for private duty nursing in the insured person's private home, for at least an 8 hour shift, by a registered nurse or licensed practical nurse who is not a member of the person's immediate family or household. Benefits will be paid up to the amount shown in the Schedule of Benefits.

5. Charges for physiotherapy given by a licensed physiotherapist.

6. Charges for ambulance service to or from a hospital.

An injury or sickness may require a person to travel by train or regularly scheduled airline to the nearest hospital where required care or treatment can be given. If so, charges incurred for such travel will be covered. Charges incurred for private charters will not be covered.

7. Charges for:

- anesthetics and their administration
- x-ray services
- lab tests and services
- preventive mammography and cytologic screening
- use of radium and radioactive isotopes
- oxygen
- blood and blood plasma (to the extent not replaced by donors)
- drugs which by law may only be dispensed with a prescription.

8. Charges to buy, rent, repair or maintain:

- artificial limbs
- artificial eyes
- crutches
- wheel chairs
- other medical equipment, appliances and supplies.

Health Insurance Policy Imaged Example (*continued*)

EXCESS MAJOR MEDICAL BENEFITS (Continued)

COVERED CHARGES (Continued)

9. Charges made for hospice care, as follows:

- charges made by a hospice, up to the lesser of:

- 185 consecutive days of confinement per benefit period, or
- $25,000 while insured; and

- charges for respite care, up to five days per occurrence.

- charges for:
- counselling of the terminally ill person and his family, up to a combined maximum of $500, and
- bereavement counselling to the family of the terminally ill person, up to a combined maximum of $250

HOSPICE means an entity licensed, approved or authorized to provide inpatient medical relief of pain and supportive care to terminally ill persons. Such entity must have on its premises:

- organized facilities to care for and treat terminally ill persons, and
- a paid staff of medical professionals to supervise such care and treatment.

RESPITE CARE means hospital confinement in lieu of home hospice care in order to give temporary relief to a caregiver who regularly assists with home care.

FAMILY means the parent, spouse, sibling or child of the terminally ill person.

A physician must certify that the terminally ill person has a life expectancy of 6 months or less.

10. Charges made for home health care, as follows:

- part-time (less than an 8 hour shift) or intermittent home nursing care by, or supervised by, a registered nurse
- part-time (less than an 8 hour shift) or intermittent home health aide services which mainly care for the patient

(PART-TIME or INTERMITTENT CARE also means full-time or 24 hour services medically required for not more than 3 days.)

- occupational, speech or physical therapy
- medical social work
- special meals and nutritional services.

HOME HEALTH CARE means excess major medical given to a person at his home and prescribed by his physician. The plan of care must be:

- in lieu of confinement in a hospital or skilled nursing facility (as defined in Title XVIII of the Social Security Act), and
- set up and approved, in writing, by a physician and a home health care agency certified by the state department of health or as defined in title XVIII of the Social Security Act.

Benefits will be paid, up to:

- 100 home health care visits per injury or sickness, and
- $60 per visit.

Each visit by a member of a home health care team will be considered one home health care visit. Four hours of home health aide services will be considered one home health care visit.

Benefits will not be paid in excess of those that would be paid by the group policy for similar charges incurred while hospitalized.

MM-3

Limitations

Benefits will be paid for covered charges incurred for the medical services shown below **only** to the extent described below.

dental care, treatment or surgery

Charges for these services will be covered only if:

1. they result from an injury to the jaw or natural teeth;
2. the injury is caused by an accident which occurs while the person is insured; and
3. such services are rendered within 6 months of the accident.

Health Insurance Policy Imaged Example (*continued*)

EXCESS MAJOR MEDICAL BENEFITS (Continued)

Limitations (Continued)

treatment for alcoholism and drug addiction

For these services, only the following charges will be covered:

charges incurred while the person is a resident patient in a licensed facility which has a program for inpatient treatment of alcoholism or drug abuse based on a written plan approved and supervised by a physician and which has affiliation with a hospital which has an established patient referral system, up to:

- 30 days per confinement, or
- 60 days while insured.

Successive confinements will be considered one confinement unless the person resumes the normal activities of a person of like age and sex, with like occupation or retired status.

treatment for psychiatric, mental, nervous or emotional disorders

For these services, only charges incurred while the person is hospitalized, up to the maximum shown in the Schedule of Benefits will be covered.

transplant surgery

Benefits for charges incurred by a donor(s) for transplant surgery will be limited to the maximum shown in the Schedule of Benefits.

MM-4

PREGNANCY BENEFITS

No pregnancy benefits will be paid by this section, except as described on page P.

CHARGES NOT COVERED

1 Charges to buy or rent:

- air conditioners
- air purifiers
- motorized transportation equipment
- escalators or elevators in private homes
- eye glass frames or lenses
- hearing aids
- swimming pools or supplies for them
- general exercise equipment.

2 Charges incurred after a person's insurance ends, regardless of when the injury or sickness occurred. However, excess major medical benefits may be provided as described in the Benefits After Insurance Ends provision on the next page.

3 Charges for a routine physical exam, except charges for preventive mammography and cytologic screening.

MM-5(Q)

BENEFITS AFTER INSURANCE ENDS

If a person's insurance ends while he is totally disabled, excess major medical benefits will be paid for covered charges if:

- they are incurred to treat the injury or sickness which caused the total disability
- they are incurred within 12 months after insurance ends
- total disability is continuous from the day insurance ends to the day the charge is incurred, and
- the person is not covered under another group plan which would replace this Excess Major Medical insurance program

MM-6(Q)

—9—

E-160,071

Health Insurance Policy Imaged Example (*continued*)

PRE-EXISTING CONDITIONS PROVISIONS FOR EXCESS MAJOR MEDICAL BENEFITS

PRE-EXISTING CONDITION means an injury or sickness for which a person:

- incurred charges
- received medical treatment
- consulted a physician, or
- took prescribed drugs

within 12 months before he became insured under a given benefit section of the group policy.

In spite of any other provision of the group policy:

No charges incurred for a pre-existing condition will be considered covered charges under a benefit section **until:** → (B)

1. the person has not:

- incurred charges
- received medical treatment
- consulted a physician, or
- taken prescribed drugs

for such condition, or any complication of it, for 6 continuous months, while insured; or

2. the person stays insured under such benefit section for 24 continuous months.

PEC

SPECIAL PROVISIONS FOR GROUPS TAKEN OVER FROM A PRIOR PLAN

These special provisions apply **only** to those persons who were insured under the Prior Plan.

EXCEPTION TO THE PRE-EXISTING CONDITIONS PROVISION

The requirements of the provision will be waived.

CREDIT FOR THE DEDUCTIBLE

For the deductible accumulation period in which such person becomes insured, the deductible will be reduced by the covered charges which were:

- incurred while insured by the prior plan, and
- used to reduce the deductible for that plan during the deductible accumulation period.

The deductible accumulation period under the group policy will be reduced by the amount of time applied toward the deductible accumulation period under the prior plan.

BENEFIT RULES

For insured persons who were totally disabled on the date the prior plan terminated and remain continuously totally disabled

No benefits will be payable under the group policy with respect to the injury or sickness which caused the total disability for the period of time that Extended Insurance benefits are payable under the prior plan.

After such period of time, benefits will be payable for such injury or sickness provided:

- the benefit period has not been exhausted;
- the insured person satisfies any excess of the deductible requirement under the group policy over the deductible under the prior plan; and
- the Maximum benefits imposed under the Prior Plan have not been paid. This includes benefits paid under the prior plan plus any benefits paid under the group policy.

If the benefit period has been exhausted, no benefits will be paid under the group policy for that injury or sickness.

Health Insurance Policy Imaged Example (*continued*)

SPECIAL PROVISIONS FOR GROUPS TAKEN OVER FROM A PRIOR PLAN (Continued)

For insured persons who were not totally disabled, but were in the process of satisfying the deductible or receiving benefits under the prior plan

Benefits will be payable with respect to the injury or sickness which led to the payment of benefits or accumulation of the deductible provided:

- the benefit period has not been exhausted;
- the insured person satisfies any excess of the deductible requirement under the group policy over the deductible under the prior plan; and
- the Maximum benefits imposed under the Prior Plan have not been paid. This includes benefits paid under the prior plan plus any benefits paid under the group policy.

If the benefit period has been exhausted, no benefits will be paid under the group policy for that injury or sickness.

TOG-2

GENERAL EXCLUSIONS

No excess major medical benefits will be paid by the group policy for charges incurred for treatment which:

1 is given after a person's insurance ends, regardless of when the injury or sickness occurred.

However, excess major medical benefits may be provided in the Benefits After Insurance Ends provision of a given benefit section.

2 is not essential for the necessary care or treatment of the injury or sickness involved.

NECESSARY CARE OR TREATMENT means care, treatment, services or supplies which are:

- recommended, approved or certified by a physician as necessary and reasonable, and
- commonly viewed by the American Medical Association as being proper treatment.

"Necessary care or treatment" **does not mean** care, treatment, services or supplies which are:

- to train a person for a job or to educate him, or
- experimental in nature.

3 would be given free of charge if the person was not insured.

However, excess major medical benefits **will be paid** for covered charges incurred by a state for medical assistance to an insured person under Title XIX of the Social Security Act of 1965.

4 results from a war or an act of war.

5 results from intentionally self-inflicted injury.

6. results from committing a felony.

7 is given by a person's spouse or his or his spouse's father, mother, son, daughter, brother or sister.

8. is given by a person's employer or an employee of such employer.

GE(Q)

E-160,071

For health insurance especially, it is important to look beyond the basic elements of the plan to evaluate what coverage it will provide. The following set of questions should help you evaluate each traditional indemnity health insurance plan for basic coverage issues. Answer each question based on the content of the plan materials you have in writing, and make notes in the left margin. If you cannot answer the question based on summary plan information, note that in the margin and obtain the necessary information from your plan administrator.

This evaluation sheet should be attached to your worksheet and included with each policy. Although the complete contents of these evaluations will not be included in the spreadsheets you will create in the next exercise, you should make sure the content of each policy evaluation is available when you consider planning for risk elements in the last exercise.

Health Insurance Policy Evaluation: Indemnity Major Medical and Hospitalization (Part B)

1. What is and is not covered? Are all necessary categories of expenses covered? Is there coverage for durable medical equipment? Home health care? Rehabilitation care? Mental health benefits? What limits exist for emergency care?
2. How much of the hospital charges or doctor's fee are covered? Is coverage based on "usual, customary and reasonable" (UCR) or the amount actually billed? For example, if your plan covers 80% of the UCR amount and your physician charges more than that amount, the insurer will not pay 80% of the physician's bill. It will pay 80% of the UCR amount, and you will have to pay the deductible plus the entire difference between your physician's fee and the UCR amount. How is UCR determined?
3. To what extent are you personally responsible for any items deemed not covered or only partially covered by the insurer? Does the catastrophic stop-loss measure include items that are not covered but medically necessary in addition to covered charges, or only out-of-pocket expenses for covered charges? If the latter, your out-of-pocket expenses could easily far exceed the catastrophic stop-loss stated in the policy.
4. Are any benefits based on a "formulary" (e.g., coverage only for a list of prescriptions or durable medical equipment), or are they based on medical necessity alone?
5. Does the policy coverage extend to foreign countries while traveling?

Self-Insured Employer and HMO Plan Health Insurance Worksheet Instructions

Effective Date of Insurance: This is the date on which coverage became effective.

Preexisting Condition Limitation (if any): List any exclusion used by insurers to avoid paying for care to treat a medical disease or condition that was or could have been diagnosed before enrollment under the policy. Quote the actual policy language here.

Preexisting Condition Waiting Period (if any): List any period of time that must elapse after policy enrollment before the insurer will pay for care to treat a medical disease or condition that was or could have been diagnosed before enrollment, as defined by the plan.

Date of Expiration of Waiting Period: Calculate—Effective date of insurance, moved forward for the waiting period, if any.

Annual Premium: The total amount you pay for the policy in a year. If you make monthlypayments, multiply your monthly premium by 12; if quarterly, multiply by 4.

Name, Address, and Phone Number of Administrator: List any pertinent information to help you contact the insurance administrator, including for treatment grievances or appeals. Also list any necessary group affiliation information here.

Policy or Identification Numbers: The number used by the company to identify your particular insurance contract.

Identity and Birthdate(s) of Insured(s): Name all persons insured, and list their birthdates.

Date Coverage Ceases (if based on insured's age, for each insured): If your insurance policy pays until a particular age (e.g., 65), calculate the date on which coverage ceases based on the insured's current age.

Event Upon Which Coverage Ceases (if based on insured's affiliation or employment): If your insurance policy covers you only while you are employed or a member of some organization, note that limitation. Also, if your employment must be full-time or a minimum number of hours per week, note this fact along with how the plan defines eligibility.

Standard Annual Deductible: List the amount the insured must pay before the insurer begins to pay toward the cost of health services otherwise covered under the plan.

Catastrophic (or "Stop-Loss") Out-of-Pocket Expense Limitation: List the maximum covered out-of pocket expenses that the policy requires you to pay before it will cover the rest of your insured expenses.

Any Other Contributions or Copayments: List any other expenses, portions of expenses, or contributions of covered items that your policy requires you to pay.

Maximum Lifetime Coverage: The maximum number of dollars that your insurance company is required to spend during the life of your policy. Look for a lifetime maximum of at least $1 million. More is better. The more people covered by your plan, the higher this number should be.

Index Identification is the identifier you assigned to the policy in the earlier exercise.

Health Insurance Policy Worksheet: Self-Insured Employer & HMO Plan (Part A)

Today's Date: ____________________

Effective Date of Insurance: ____________________

Preexisting Condition Limitations: ____________________

If Preexisting Condition Waiting Period, Date of Expiration of Period: ________

____

Annual Premium (12 times monthly or 4 times quarterly): ____________

____

Name, Address, and Phone Number of Administrator and Group Affiliation (if any) ____________________

____

Policy or Identification Numbers: ____________________

Identity and Birthdate(s) of Insured(s): ____________________

Date Coverage Ceases (if based on insured's age, for each insured): ________

____

Event Upon Which Coverage Ceases (if based on insured's affiliation or employment): ____________________

Standard Annual Deductible: ____________________

Catastrophic (or "stop-loss") Out-of-Pocket Expense Limitation: ________

____

Any Other Contributions or Copayments: ____________________

____

Maximum Lifetime Coverage: ____________________

____

Index Identification: ____________________

____

Health Insurance Policy Evaluation: Self-Insured Employer and HMO Plan (Part B)

Evaluate your plan for basic coverage issues. Answer each question based on the content of the plan materials you have in writing. If you cannot answer the question based on plan information, note that in the margin.

- Is your primary physician board-certified or eligible? How many of the plan's physicians are board-certified or eligible? Look for at least 70%.
- What is the policy for referral to specialists? How complicated is the process, and how long does it take?
- What physicians and hospitals are part of the network? Is the plan affiliated with a good hospital and accredited or government-qualified? Get a complete listing, and make sure you have a range of choices. A good rule of thumb is three specialists in each field.
- How strong is the organization and management? What is the plan's medical loss ratio? This ratio tells you how much is spent on actual care. For example, a ratio of 95 means 95 cents out of every dollar is spent on care. The higher the ratio, the better. Look for a ratio in excess of 85.
- What is the physician turnover rate in the plan? Regardless of the reason for leaving, it causes disruption in the plan. Look for a turnover rate lower than 10%.
- Is the organization in sound financial health? How long has it done business in your area? A track record of three or more years is recommended.
- Can you choose your own doctor? Can you select a specialist as your primary physician?
- Is routine care given by a physician or delegated to others?
- How are physicians in the plan reimbursed? Are there any incentives that would lead physicians to skimp on care? You should know if they are being paid a set yearly fee for your care or a fee every time they see you. You need to know if the plan rewards providers for not giving or authorizing care, or penalizes them for giving or authorizing care.
- How long does it take to get an appointment?
- Does it offer a full range of preventive health services?
- What is not covered (e.g., durable medical equipment, medications, home nursing care, rehab care)?
- What is the preexisting condition policy?
- How much does it cost?
- What happens if a physician or other health service is needed outside the plan? What out-of-network benefits, if any, are provided? Do you have a point-of-service option?
- In case of disagreement, what is the procedure? Your plan should have a formal appeals procedure, in which your objections are reviewed by different, but at least equally qualified, personnel. This is especially important in plans that are employer-sponsored and covered by ERISA. How soon can you expect a decision? Are you guaranteed a decision on your appeal?

- How carefully does the plan listen to its patients? Does it use regular surveys and evaluations of physicians, and reward doctors who get good reviews?
- What provisions has your plan made for coverage while you travel? Does it have reciprocal arrangements?
- Can you get emergency care without first calling an HMO number? Does the HMO defiine an emergency in such a way that an average person's idea of an "emergency" is covered?
- What kind of confidentiality provisions for medical records are provided?

Health Insurance Policy Worksheet: Medicare (Traditional)[15]

Effective Date of Insurance: (note: this is *not necessarily* the same as the date of social security eligibility)

Hospitalization: 90 Days of hospitalization per benefit period; 60 extra lifetime reserve days

190 days lifetime limit for psychiatric inpatient benefits
2002 Deductible for first 60-day benefit period = $812
Between 60–90 days, 2002 coinsurance per day = $203
Lifetime Reserve 60 days, 2002 coinsurance per day = $406
Between 21–100 days in skilled nursing facility, 2002 coinsurance per day = $101.50

Part A 2002 Premium (For Medicare Full Buy-In): $319 per month; (For Medicare Partial Buy-In): $175 per month

Part B 2002 Monthly Premium: (set by law) $54.00/month

Part B Deductible = $100 per year

Part B Medical Insurance Pays 80% of "Approved Charges" for:

Physicians, Outpatient Hospital Treatment, X-ray, Injections (not self-administered)

Laboratory Work, Diagnostic Tests, Ambulance, Medical Equipment, Supplies

Outpatient Physical Therapy and Speech Therapy: If received as part of treatment at physician's office: 80%; If received at therapists office or at your home: $400 per year, unless you are "confined to home," in which case it will pay 100%

Medicare does NOT pay for self-administered prescription medications

Buy-ins: For noneligible individuals, age 65 and over[16] the Medicare Part A (Hospital Insurance) Premium for 2002 is $319 per month. (Note: this premium is only paid by individuals with less than 30 quarters of Medicare covered employment.) For individuals with 30-39 quarters of Medicare covered employment, the Part A buy-in premium for 2002 is reduced to $175.00 per month.

---

[15] Other Medicare options may be available to you, depending on where you live. Such options could include a Medicare HMO plan, a Medicare Medical Savings Account (MSA) plan, or a Medicare private Fee-for-Service plan. For updated Medicare benefits information, see the internet at http://www.medicare.gov/basics/amounts2002.asp.

[16] Several legislative proposals in Congress would decrease the Medicare buy-in age eligibility from 65 to 55, thus making medicare available to more ineligible early retirees. It is unclear whether those retirees would also have access to Medigap as the states control availability of such policies. As with nonelderly disabled Medicare recipients, Medigap eligibility varies state-by-state.

Medigap Policy Federal Requirements (Summary)

Either all or none of the Part A hospital deductible

Coinsurance for days 61 through 90 and 91 through 150 at prevailing rates

Blood deductible unless blood is replaced

At least 20% of Medicare approved Part B coinsurance after annual deductible

Guarantee renewability

Cover preexisting conditions after maximum waiting period of 6 months

Long-Term Care Policy Worksheet Instructions[17]

Index ID is the identifier you assigned to the policy in the earlier exercise.

Annual Premium is the total amount you pay for the policy in a year. If you make monthly payments, multiply your monthly premium by 12; if quarterly, multiply by 4; if biweekly, by 26.

Level Premium is a premium that does not change over time.

Waiver of Premium is a policy provision that guarantees that the insurance will continue in force without the payment of premiums after you have established that you are disabled, as defined by the policy, and continue during the entire term of disability.

Insurer's Financial Strength Rating must be obtained by either telephone or the Internet. Use the instructions contained on pages 5–6. You may use any of the raters listed in there, but make sure you obtain the rating for the actual company that underwrites your policy.

Contact information for the insurance company should be located on the policy. If not, call your agent and obtain it for your records.

Contact information for your agent or group affiliates, if any, should be stored with your policy. If not, write it down and store it with your policy.

Policy or Identification Numbers: The number used by the company to identify your particular insurance contract to the insurance company.

Identity and Birth date(s) of Insured(s): Name all persons insured, and list their birthdates.

Noncancellable and guaranteed renewable: Examine your policy to see if you have the right to renew your policy despite claims made, and circle yes/no on the worksheet; also see if you have protection against cancellation by the insurance company despite claims made, and circle yes/no on the worksheet (which, by the way, also protects against premium increases).

Nonforfeiture Benefits: examine your policy to see if a form of a cash value is paid up during the life of the policy, and if it is available if you surrender the policy. If your policy accrues such values, it has a nonforfeiture benefit. Circle yes/no on the worksheet.

Adult Day Care Benefit: This is a benefit for a special community-based adult day care center. Adult day care provides a structured, supervised, social environment to support care needs. The adult day care center must be state-licensed or certified. Circle yes/no on the worksheet.

Inflation Benefit: This is a benefit that will allow your insurance policy to keep up with increasing costs over time. Check you policy to see if it has an annual percentage increase in the benefits to keep up with increasing long-term care

[17] An example of a completed worksheet for a long-term care policy, cross-referenced to the policies, is included at the end of these instructions.

costs (circle yes/no) and, if so, note what the annual increase percentage is, and whether it is tied to an index (and, if so, what index).

Daily Home Care Benefits: These are benefits that are provided in your home, as opposed to a facility such as a nursing home. Note the amount of the benefits and whether there are any limitations on the type of services covered or conditions under which such services will be provided.[18]

Home Care Requiring Hospital Stay First: Note (yes/no) whether your policy requires as a condition for eligibility for home care benefits whether you must commence long-term service upon discharge from a hospital or nursing home.

Daily Nursing Home Benefits: Note the amount of the benefits and whether the policy fails to include coverage for (1) skilled care, (2) intermediate care, (3) custodial care, (4) sheltered care, or (5) assisted living.

Waiting Period: Note whether your policy has a waiting period and, if so for how long.

Maximum Benefits: Note whether your policy has a maximum benefit limitation for a single covered period of care; also whether there is a maximum lifetime benefit for all covered periods of care.

---

[18] Home care benefits should cover registered nurses (RNs); licensed practical nurses (LPNs); physical, respiratory, and speech therapy; personal care attendants; chore services; meal preparation; adult day care; respite care; shopping; and assistance with grooming and dressing.

Long-Term Care Policy Worksheet

Today's Date and Index ID of Policy: ____________________

Annual Premium (12 times monthly or 26 times biweekly): ____________________

____

Does Premium stay level for life?: ____________________

Does Policy Have a Waiver of Premium Provision?: ____________________

____

Name, Address, Phone Number, and Financial Strength Rating of Insurance Company: ____________________

____

Name, Address, and Phone Number of Agent or Group Affiliation (if applicable): ____________________

____

Policy or Identification Numbers: ____________________

Identity and Birth date(s) of Insured(s): ____________________

Is Policy Noncancellable/Guaranteed Renewable for Life? ____________________

____

Does Policy Include Nonforfeiture Benefits? ____________________

Does Policy Pay Adult Day Care Benefits? ____________________

Does Policy Pay Inflation Protection?: ____________________

____

Daily Home Care Benefit: ____________________

Does Home Care Require Nursing Home or Hospital Stay First?: ____________________

Daily Nursing Home Benefit: ____________________

Waiting Period: ____________________

Maximum Benefits—one stay/all stays ____________________

____

As with health insurance, it is important to evaluate what coverage long-term care insurance will provide to determine adequacy. The following set of questions should help you evaluate long-term care policies. Answer each question based on the content of the plan materials you have in writing, and make notes in the left margin.

This evaluation sheet should be attached to your worksheet and included with each policy. Although the complete contents of these evaluations will not be included in the spreadsheets you will create in the next exercise, you should make sure the content of each policy evaluation is available when you consider planning for risk elements in the last exercise.

Long-Term Care Policy Evaluation

- Are daily benefit amounts based on an indemnity (meaning that a specific amount is stated) or on reimbursement of amounts charged? Reimbursement policies are more likely to provide the range and level of services that will be needed; indemnity policies purchased today may provide nowhere near the level of coverage needed in the future.
- Does nursing home care include skilled, intermediate, and custodial care, as well as sheltered care and assisted living?
- Does home care include RNs; LPNs; LVNs; physical, respiratory, and speech therapy; personal care attendants; chore services; meal preparation; adult day care; respite care; shopping; and assistance with grooming and dressing? Does home care require a skilled component or is there provision for custodial care by itself? Try to avoid policies that require a skilled component, as this seriously limits the availability of home versus institutional care.
- If medical necessity is required, is it determined by your own physician or someone else?
- Does the policy require prior hospitalization for benefits? These provisions should be avoided because they seriously curtail the coverage for needed benefits; only a portion of needs for care arise immediately after hospitalization.
- Is the policy guaranteed renewable for life? Without this clause, nothing prevents the company from canceling the policy or changing benefits.
- Look for a policy in which the premium amount is based on age at time of enrollment; also, look for a policy with a level premium.
- Make sure the policy is portable, meaning that the benefits are available wherever you are. This is particularly true if you like to travel or live away from your extended family (and might choose to relocate).
- Look for policies that allow an alternative plan of care; for example, if a policy would pay for an alternative setting if a nursing home confinement would otherwise be required. Under such circumstances, for example, the care might include payment for home modifications and medical equipment.
- Make sure your policy has a waiver of premium so that you will no longer have to worry about paying premiums while you are receiving benefits.
- Also look for a bed reservation benefit, meaning a policy provision that will continue to pay the nursing home in order to reserve your bed there should you become hospitalized.
- Does the policy have ample inflation protection? If not, you may discover that a facility you choose could one day become unaffordable within the terms of your insurance benefits.
- Make sure if you have an indemnity policy that the benefit amount is sufficient to cover actual local long-term care cost, with adequate inflation protection to cover cost increases as well.
- Make sure that the policy coverage period is your lifetime.
- Make sure that the plan covers Alzheimer's disease.

- Make sure that the plan covers preexisting conditions as of its effective date or that the clause is not an *exclusion* (just a waiting period) and that you have an alternative means of paying for care during the preexisting condition waiting period.
- Make sure the insurer has an adequate financial strength rating.
- Look for a plan that offers a choice of deductible periods (to meet your specific needs based on your other resources).

EXERCISE 2
Creating the Spreadsheets

Your next task is to compile information about each policy in a format that will allow your total coverage for each policy type to be determined and summarized. For example, the life insurance spreadsheet will help you determine the total amount of life insurance you currently carry. Based on the information you have compiled in your insurance worksheets, you should be able to fill in the following spreadsheets. Each insurance policy (and therefore each worksheet you completed earlier) will provide information for one horizontal line on the summarizing spreadsheet. As with the worksheets, examples are provided in the spreadsheets to guide you in your entries. If you need more lines than are provided, you should copy the spreadsheet and use more than one page for each type of insurance. Although these spreadsheets are not exhaustive, they are a basic tool that you can use in the final exercise to evaluate the adequacy of your portfolio and devise an action plan. A separate spreadsheet should be compiled for each member of the family. Unless one or more children or other dependents has special needs, coverages, or considerations, dependent children can be treated as a group on a single spreadsheet.

Life Insurance Spreadsheet Instructions

Index ID: This identifier should be taken directly from the worksheet for the policy.

Face Amount: This amount should be taken directly from the worksheet and is the same as the *Face Amount of Policy.*

Additional Death Benefits: This amount is the same as *additional death benefits as of today* and should be taken directly from the worksheet.

Total Death Benefits: This gross amount is calculated based on the terms of the policy. For a rough estimate, add *Face Amount* and *Additional Death Benefits,* above.

Loans: This is the same as *Loans Outstanding as of Today* and should be taken directly from the worksheet.

Net Cash Value: This refers to the amount of cash value currently available based on the terms of the policy. For a rough estimate, subtract *Loans from Total Death Benefits.*

Living Benefits: If this provision exists, it should be summarized from the worksheet.

Issue Date: This is the same as *Date Issued* and should be taken from the worksheet.

Type of Policy: This refers to subtype of policy (e.g., term or whole) and should be taken from the worksheet.

Annual Premium: This should be taken directly from the worksheet.

Rating: This refers to the financial strength rating of the insurer and should be taken from the worksheet.

Policy Number: This should be taken from the worksheet.

Insured's Birthdate: This should be taken directly from the worksheet.

Beneficiary: This name or names should be taken directly from the worksheet.

Term Decrease Formula: If this is a term life policy, quote the formula by which coverage decreases with age, as stated on the worksheet.

Term Cessation Date: If this is a term policy, specify the date on which coverage will cease based on age, as stated on the worksheet. You may wish to compare this with your Social Security full retirement eligibility date. See Appendix 4.

■ SUMMARIZING THE SPREADSHEET

At the bottom of the spreadsheet, record two sets of some summary values. You should separate employment-based insurance (whether from yourself or from your spouse) from other sources of insurance. Make one summary for each type (employment-based and nonemployment-based). Summarize both as follows:

1. Add all of the amounts in the column labeled *Total Death Benefits,* and record this amount on the bottom line. To mark it as a summary, you might want to double underline the amount.
2. Add all of the amounts in the column labeled *Net Cash Value,* and record this amount on the bottom line. To mark it as a summary, you might want to double underline the amount.

Use the decrease formulas to determine how much your life insurance will decrease in terms of dollars and when (if) it will finally completely expire. Pay special attention to your age on the cessation date, and compare this with your Social Security full retirement eligibility date. See Appendix 4.

Life Insurance Spreadsheet

Date Created:

Insured:

Index ID#	Face Amount	Addt'l Death Benefits	Total Death Benefits	Loans	Net Cash Value	Endowment or Living Benefits
Column A	Column B	Column C	Column D	Col E	Column F	Column G

(continued)

Life Insurance Spreadsheet

Page 2

Insured:

Type of Policy	Annual Premium	Rating	Policy #	Insured B/D	Beneficiary	Term: Decrease Formula	Term: Cessation Date
Column H	Column I	Col J	Col K	Column L	Column M	Column N	Column O

Disability Insurance Spreadsheet Instructions

Index ID: This identifier should be taken directly from the worksheet for the policy.

Premium: Refers to the annual premium from the worksheet, including any contributions made by an employer if it is an employer plan.

Rating: Refers to the financial strength rating for the underwriting insurance company from the worksheet for the policy.

Monthly Benefits: Refers to the amount or formula on the policy worksheet. For purposes of the spreadsheet, if the amount is a formula, record the amount of the benefit if you were to become disabled today.

Adjustments: Refers to any offsets or cost-of-living adjustments, as listed on your worksheet.

Net Benefit: This is the calculated after-tax amount on the worksheet and should be taken from the worksheet.

Percentage of Month Income: This refers to the percentage of monthly income and is the second calculated amount reported on the worksheet after net benefit. Take this amount directly from the worksheet.

Partial Benefits: Take this information directly from the worksheet.

Policy Term: This is the same as *Term of Policy* on the worksheet and should be recorded directly from the worksheet.

Elimination: This is the same thing as *Elimination Period* on the worksheet and should be recorded directly from the worksheet.

Definition of Disability: This should be recorded in summary format from the worksheet. This is the same as the *Initial Definition of Disability* on the worksheet and should be recorded summarily, such as "own occupation" or "unable to hold job."

Later Definition of Disability: This should also be recorded in summary format from the worksheet. This is the same as the *Further Definition of Disability* on the worksheet and should be recorded summarily as well. If there is no later definition, leave this space blank.

Coverage Ceases Event: This includes the contents of both *Date Coverage Ceases* and *Coverage Ceases Event* from the worksheet. Record the item that will cause coverage to cease from the worksheet.

■ SUMMARIZING THE SPREADSHEET

At the bottom of the spreadsheet, record two sets of some summary values. You should separate employment-based insurance (whether from yourself or from your spouse) from other sources of insurance. Make one summary for each type. Summarize both as follows:

1. Add all of the amounts in the column labeled *Net Benefit,* and record this amount on the bottom line. To mark it as a summary, you might want to double underline the amount.
2. Add all of the amounts in the column labeled *Percentage of Month Income,* and record the total percentage of monthly income (after taxes). To mark it as a summary, you might want to double underline the amount.

Disability Insurance Spreadsheet

Date Created:

Insured: Birthdate of Insured:

Index ID#	Premium	Rating	Monthly Benefits	Adjustments: Offsets, COLAs	Net Benefit	% of Month Income	Partial Benefits	Policy #
Column A	Column B	Col C	Column D	Column E	Column F	Column G	Column H	Col I

(continued)

Disability Insurance Spreadsheet

Page 2

Insured:

Policy Term	Elimination	Definition of Disability	Later Definition of Disability	Coverage Ceases Event
Column J	Column K	Column L	Column M	Column N

Health Insurance Spreadsheet Instructions

Index ID: This should be taken directly from the worksheet.

Premium: This is the same as *Annual Premium* and should be taken directly from the worksheet.

Rating: This is the same as the *insurer financial strength rating* and should be taken directly from the worksheet.

Preexisting Limits: This is the same as the *Preexisting Condition Limitations* and should be taken directly from the worksheet. Additionally, note any health conditions excluded from coverage by virtue of this limitation.

Deductible: This is the same as the *Annual Deductible* and should be taken directly from the worksheet. If not applicable (for example, HMO, VA, or worker's compensation coverage), note this fact.

Stop Loss: This is the same as the *Catastrophic Out-Of-Pocket Expense Limitation* and should be taken directly from the worksheet. If this is not applicable, note this fact.

Copayments: This is the same as *Any Other Contributions or Copayments* and should be taken directly from the worksheet. If this is not applicable, note this fact.

Lifetime Limit: This is the same as the worksheet and should be entered directly from the worksheet.

Policy #: This should be taken directly from the worksheet.

Policy Coverage Notes: You should note any items from your evaluation worksheet (Part B) that are significant based on the level of coverage you think you need in order to incorporate them into your final action plan.

Coverage Ceases Event: This includes the contents of both *Date Coverage Ceases* and *Event Upon Which Coverage Ceases* from the worksheet. Record the item(s) that will cause coverage to cease from the worksheet.

Health Insurance Spreadsheet

Date Created:

Insured: Birthdate of Insured:

Index ID#	Premium	Rating	Pre-Existing Limits	Deductible	Stop-Loss	Co-payments	Lifetime Limit
Column A	Column B	Col C	Column D	Column E	Column F	Column G	Column H

Health Insurance Spreadsheet

Page 2

Insured:

Policy #	Policy Coverage Notes	Coverage Ceases Event
Col I	Column J	

Long-Term Care Insurance Spreadsheet Instructions

Index ID: This should be taken directly from the worksheet.

Premium: This is the same as *Annual Premium* and should be taken directly from the worksheet.

Rating: This is the same as the financial strength rating of the insurance company and should be taken directly from the worksheet.

Daily Nursing Home: Summarize the actual daily nursing home benefit here from the answer on your worksheet.

Daily Home Care: Summarize the actual daily home care benefit here from the answer on your worksheet.

Stay Required First?: This is for your answer to the question on the worksheet about requirements for a nursing home or hospital stay as a prerequisite for benefits. You should record that answer here as well.

Waiting Period: This answer should be taken directly from your worksheet.

Benefit Limits: This refers to *Maximum Benefits* from the worksheet, and that information should be recorded here as well.

Policy #: This should be taken directly from your worksheet.

Renewable for Life?: This is for your answer to the question on the worksheet about whether the policy is noncancellable/guaranteed renewable for life, and that information should be recorded here as well.

Premium Waiver?: This is for your answer to the question on the worksheet about whether the policy has a waiver of premium provision, and that information should be recorded here as well.

Nonforfeiture?: This is for your answer to the question on the worksheet about nonforfeiture benefits, and it should be recorded here as well.

Level Premium: This is for your answer to the question on the worksheet, and it should be recorded here as well.

Coverage Notes: You should note any items from your evaluation worksheet (Part B) that are significant based on the level of coverage you think you need in order to incorporate them into your final action plan.

Long-Term Care Insurance Spreadsheet

Date Created:

Insured: Birthdate of Insured:

Index ID#	Premium	Rating	Daily Nursing Home	Daily Home Care	Stay Required First?	Waiting Period	Benefit Limits	Policy #
Column A	Col B	Col C	Column D	Column E	Column F	Column G	Column H	Col I

(continued)

Long-Term Care Insurance Spreadsheet

Page 2

Insured:

Renewable for Life?	Premium Waiver?	Nonforfeiture?	Level Premium?	Coverage Notes
Column J	Column K	Column L	Column M	Column N

EXERCISE 3

Evaluate and Analyze Your Insurance Needs

Now that you know what insurance coverage you have, and it is summarized in a fairly usable, organized way on your spreadsheets, you need to set about determining what your actual insurance needs are in order to compare what you have with what you actually need. Most people falsely assume that they should evaluate their insurance needs by type of coverage, then try to determine gaps in coverage also based on the *type* of coverage. Although that is the way we have organized the records and the spreadsheets, in reality the information on the spreadsheet is merely a *starting point* for a much more probing and multidimensional analysis. Instead of coverage type, the adequacy of insurance coverage should be evaluated by *risk category.* In devising a protection plan, you must identify each element of risk, given the position, expectations, and obligations for each member of the family group. Based on those categories, you then evaluate how well your current portfolio as a whole covers you for those risks.

First, it is important to know what "risk" means in this context in order to understand how it is organized here. Risk means the possibility—any possibility—that events in life will not go exactly as you had planned or hoped. In its most simple terms, "risk" is everything that might go wrong. When you make a financial plan to reach a financial goal, you assume that things will pretty much be able to chug along at a particular rate and that at some given time you will reach your goal. Anything that can involuntarily distract you from reaching that goal is "risk."

If you were truly pessimistic, you could sit down for days and list all the things that could go wrong that could prevent you from reaching your financial goals. In order to be more productive in your analysis, you should think about risk in terms of the three basic strategies for dealing with it.

- First, risk can be *assumed.* That means that you make no specific plans and instead you just assume that the lumps that befall you due to risk will fall where they may. Alternatively, you may make an astute and conscious decision to assume a risk that you believe you can ameliorate given your other resources should the risk come to fruition. For example, you may have a wealthy family who can simply pay the bills if you have a major health problem, and therefore the contents of your coverage may not be too important.
- Second, risk can be *avoided.* In this case you may take particular steps to make sure that if a certain bad event occurs, you will not be held responsible for it. You have probably seen things such as "hold harmless" clauses in various contracts or leases you have signed. These are forms of avoiding risk. You can avoid some health risks by choosing not to engage in high-risk or unhealthy

activities (such as sky diving or snorkeling). If you never ride in a car, for example, you are unlikely to be involved in a car accident (except, perhaps, as a pedestrian).

- Third, risk can be *insured against.* In other words, by way of example, instead of closing your eyes to the possibility of ill health and taking your lumps, you can insure yourself against that possibility to protect your financial position should you incur medical expenses that are beyond your current means. The amount of risk insured against will dictate the remaining amount of risk that must either be assumed (and paid for) or avoided. For example if you limit your health insurance coverage to catastrophic coverage only, you will need a correspondingly larger source of savings or other ready cash to pay for uninsured health expenses as they arise.

Everyone has a risk strategy. It may not be a conscious strategy, but a strategy exists nonetheless. That is because every one of life's problems is dealt with by every person in one of the three ways described above. Some of us are more insured than others. Some of us avoid risk more than others. Some of us are very calculating in all of our financial decisions. Then again, some of us close our eyes and dive right in. The key to successful risk planning is to find a conscious mix of those approaches that provides enough protection given the reality of your means, goals, and lifestyle.

Thus, there is no single formula for determining whether all of your insurance coverage is adequate. What we will do in this exercise is to use the information you organized earlier and reorganize it into risk categories. After that is done, coverage for risk categories will be evaluated based on your own coverage in order to help you prepare your own action plan for improving your portfolio.

The list of risks devised for this exercise are broken down by type of *event* that might occur that would cause a financial loss. For example, these might include loss of life, loss of earning power, incurring hospital bills, or the like. Some chronic illness-related risk categories are loss of income, illness, and occupational risks (such as professional liability or business interruption due to disability). For each risk category, adequate and *continuous* insurance, both long-term and short-term, are discussed to assist you in creating a comprehensive plan.

This exercise requires you to fill out a single extensive worksheet that will help you identify different *categories* of risk and summarize your current insurance plans to deal with each of them. Each of these categories has been identified in the extensive risk worksheet and is given a number. The categories and subcategories of risk identified by number are certainly not exhaustive. However, they do hit the major areas in which people with chronic diseases should be well protected. The extensive worksheet only covers personal risk; it does *not* cover occupational risk, such as professional liability or business interruption. By filling in the worksheet as instructed below, you should be able to begin discovering whether you have gaps or unnecessary duplications in coverage. Based on the text analysis following creation of your worksheet, you should be able to construct a personalized action plan to shore up any gaps or duplications you currently have in your portfolio.

It is important to remember that for each category of risk you need to make sure that there is either continuous insurance coverage or other *personal* resources to cover the risk—that your coverage is not dependent on someone else's well-being, continued employment, marital status, or income; nor does it depend on your own continued well-being, continued employment, marital status, or income; also, the coverage should not cease prematurely and should cover the entire period of time necessary. Consequently, pay close attention to the instructions for each category.

Evaluation of Insurance Coverage by Risk Category

Insured:

No.	Risk Category	Subcategory	Time Period	Spreadsheet Cross References
1	***Income Loss***	During Lifetime/Due to Illness or Disability	During Elimination Period	Accumulated Savings, expressed in terms of months of expenses supportable
2		During Lifetime/Due to Illness or Disability	Initial 5 months of Disability	Personal Savings, expressed in terms of months of expenses supportable, plus Total Monthly Disabiity Benefits (column F) with less than 5 months of elimination (column K)
3		During Lifetime/Due to Illness or Disability	6 or more months if not SSDI eligible	Total Monthly Disabiity Benefits (column F) with definition of disability based on own occupation (columns L and M) for policy term (column J) [describe]
4		During Lifetime/Due to Illness or Disability	6 or more months if SSDI eligible	Total Monthly Disability Benefits (column D) with offsets (column E) until event (column N)
5		During Lifetime/Due to Illness or Disability	Subsequent Periods under Disability Plan	Total Monthly Disability Benefits (column D) with offsets (column E) until event (column N)
6		After Death		Insert total of column D in Life Insurance Spreadsheet
7		During Lifetime of Spouse	In case of disability	Total Monthly Disability Benefits (column D) with offsets (column E) until event (column N)
8		During Lifetime of Spouse	In case of unemployment	Total Monthly Disabiity Benefits (column F) with less than 5 months of elimination (column K)
9		After Death of Spouse		Insert total of column D in Life Insurance Spreadsheet for spouse
10	***Inflation***	Loss of Income/Illness or Disability	Long-Term Disability	Refer to Column E of Disability Insurance Spreadsheet
11		Loss of Income/Spouse	Long-Term Disability	Refer to Column E of Disability Insurance Spreadsheet
12	***Illness/Injury***	Major Medical/Hospital for Illness or Disability	During Employment After Diagnosis	Coverage Summarized on Health Insurance Spreadsheet [with good content evaluation]
13		Major Medical/Hospital for Illness or Disability	After Cessation of Employment Due to Disability, Social Security Eligible	Coverage Other Than Employment-Based, or Contractual Guarantee from Employer for Continued Coverage During Disability, Possibly MediGap (check state requirements to see if non-elderly eligible) [insurance from spreadsheet with good content evaluation]

14		Major Medical/Hospital for Illness or Disability	After Cessation of Employment Due to Disability, Social Security Ineligible	Coverage Other Than Employment-Based, or Contractual Guarantee from Employer for Continued Coverage During Disability [insurance from spreadsheet with good content evaluation]
15		Major Medical/Hospital for Illness or Disability	After Retirement Age*, Social Security Eligible	Coverage Other Than Employment-Based, or Contractual Guarantee from Employer for Continued Coverage During Disability, Possibly MediGap (check state requirements to see if non-elderly eligible) [insurance from spreadsheet with good content evaluation]
16		Major Medical/Hospital for Illness or Disability	After Retirement Age*, Social Security Ineligible, Medicaid Ineligible	Coverage Other Than Employment-Based, or Contractual Guarantee from Employer for Continued Coverage During Disability [insurance from spreadsheet with good content evaluation]
17		Long-Term Care	Needs Exceed Capacity of Family to Provide	Private pay, or Coverage Summarized on Long Term Care Spreadsheet [with good content evaluation]; Medicaid State Eligibility Based on Financial Resource Limitations (poverty program); need to consult elder lawyer to plan finances and estate well in advance to leave possibility of coverage open as a possibility; limited Medicare coverage

Insurance Needs Checklist (*Continued*)

No.	Summary of Present Coverage	Gaps in Coverage	Duplicate Coverage
1			
2			
3			
4			
5			
6			
7			
8			
9			
10			
11			
12			
13			

14			
15			
16			
17			

Insurance Needs Checklist (*Continued*)

No.	Action Plan
1	
2	
3	
4	
5	
6	
7	
8	
9	
10	
11	
12	
13	

14	15	16	17	

■ ANALYZING INSURANCE COVERAGE NEEDS BY RISK CATEGORY AND EVALUATION INSTRUCTIONS

For this exercise, you will use the extensive "Evaluating Insurance Coverage by Risk Category" worksheet. Based on the contents of your insurance spreadsheets and other personal financial information, you will make notes in four columns on that worksheet: (1) "summary of present coverage," where you will list your pertinent current coverage; (2) "gaps in coverage," where you will note holes or deficiencies you find to exist in your pertinent current coverage; (3) "duplicate coverage," where you will note coverage that unnecessarily overlaps, overinsures, or duplicates other pertinent current coverage; and (4) "action plan," where you will write action items based on entries in the other 3 columns in order to improve your current coverage. The discussion for this exercise includes an analysis of each risk element listed on the worksheet in numerical order and should provide you with a blueprint for forming an individualized action plan to improve your current portfolio of insurance.

Category 1: Income Loss Due to Chronic Illness During Elimination Period of Disability Insurance Plan

The "elimination period" referred to can be found on your disability insurance spreadsheet. You need to have enough personal savings to hold you over during the period of time between when you stop working and the time you actually start to receive disability insurance payments. Additionally, if your payments are delayed for any reason, you will need to be able to draw on your personal savings during that period as well, however long it may be.[19]

Consequently, this category requires you to determine how much you actually spend every month and then calculate how long your current personal savings would last if you had to live on them. If you have "tiered" elimination periods (meaning not all of your disability plans has the same elimination period), you should calculate your cash needs on this tiered basis. In other words, for example, if you have one policy with a 30-day elimination and another with a 90-day elimination, you can add the disability proceeds of the short elimination policy to determine how much of your savings you would use during the second and third months of waiting for the 90-day elimination period to elapse. Make sure to use after-tax amounts in your calculations.

Before you ever actually apply for disability benefits, you should make sure that your other affairs are also in order to provide the resources you will need, especially if they might become unavailable after you stop working. For example, you should anticipate a change in your credit worthiness after you stop working; thus, you might want to take steps to make credit available while you are still working. For example, consider refinancing your home. If interest rates are low and you have money tied up in the home, get a home equity line of credit before you lose your job.[20] If you don't have a job or a steady source of disability income,

[19] The more likely that your claim may be disputed, the more ou should be prepared for a delay in decision. This is especially true for disabilities based on intangible elements such as pain or fatigue.

[20] Get a line of credit with no annual fee. You do not need to take the proceeds for the loan— just make the funds available on a fee-free basis in case you need them later on.

it is difficult to get anybody to give you credit. Also, obtain additional low-fee or no-fee credit cards. Even though you want to make the *credit* available, you still need to avoid the *debt* if at all possible. Get out of debt as quickly as possible before the paychecks stop coming. Make a new budget to stick to the amount of after tax income you anticipate from your disability income, and plan to begin making estimated tax payments if necessary. Reallocate savings from pension plans to individual accounts. Stop stashing money in places that are difficult to tap, such as IRAs, and stop saving in annuities and volatile stocks or mutual funds; instead, use more stable and liquid funds. Determine what cash would be available on loans against any participating insurance product (such as whole life insurance).

- **Summary of Present Coverage:** Note in this category whether your current personal savings are adequate to sustain you through your elimination periods. If not, make note of the amount of your shortfall in your **Gaps in Coverage** and in your **Action Plan.**

Category 2: Income Loss Due to Chronic Illness During First Five Months of Disability

This issue is somewhat different from Category 1. The "5 months" referred to here is the minimum waiting period established by law for Social Security Disability. Even after you file for Social Security Disability benefits and receive an award, you will not receive payment for the first five months of your disability—dating from the date of application for benefits (*not* the date of onset of the disability). Thus, if Social Security is part of your disability plan, you must have enough personal savings and other disability income to help you last during these five months (for which you will never receive retroactive payments, even if your claim is eventually granted).

Although many financial experts advise you to have 6 months of household expenses in savings, for people with chronic illness for whom Social Security Disability is a real possibility, at least one year is a more realistic figure because the vast majority of people who apply for Social Security Disability benefits are turned down, and the appeals can cause quite a delay (even assuming benefits are ultimately approved).

Consequently, this category, like the last one, requires you to determine how much you actually spend every month and then calculate how long your current personal savings and disability coverage would sustain you if you had to live on those sources alone. For this category, if your future disability is predictable, you may want to consider using Credit Life and Disability insurance to stretch your cash resources (see discussion under Action Plan later).

- **Summary of Present Coverage:** Note in this category whether your current personal savings and disability income would be adequate to sustain you for at least one year. Depending on how much you need to preserve death benefits in your life insurance (see Category 6), if you have whole life insurance you may be able to draw loans against cash values in that insurance to help you during this time because under many policies the loans do not have to be paid back during your lifetime.[21] If you do not have enough resources to

[21] Be sure to check your own policy terms.

sustain you during this time, make note of the amount of your shortfall in **Gaps in Coverage** and in your **Action Plan.** If your disability coverage exceeds your needs, note the amount of the excess in **Duplicate Coverage** and in your **Action Plan.**

Category 3: Income Loss Due to Chronic Illness After 6 Months of Disability If Not Eligible for SSDI

This category requires you to consider whether your income replacement through disability insurance would be adequate to sustain you over the long term. Is the amount of disability income after taxes sufficient? Will the entire income source last until your retirement age? If necessary, will it help you generate savings sufficient to fully fund a retirement account that will last through retirement? Will it keep up with inflation? If you partially recover, will you collect enough in disability benefits to compensate for the loss of regular working income?

In addition to concerns about the amount of income that is actually replaced by your insurance, you need to make sure that your disability insurance is designed to carry you through your entire period of disability (until you reach retirement age). If your insurance ceases before you reach retirement age (see your spreadsheet) or if there is a gap between the cessation date and your Social Security retirement age (see discussion earlier), you will need to have some other form of income for that interim period. Also, if your current health insurance is employment-based, you should be thinking about where you will obtain your health insurance during this time as well as after retirement if the employer does not contractually guarantee continued health coverage throughout your entire disability and after retirement, or if your employer-provided coverage is pared back over time.

Another important point to remember about disability insurance is that taxation depends on who pays the premium. If you have employment-sponsored insurance and the employer pays the premium, the proceeds will be taxable, which effectively reduces their value. The proceeds will be nontaxable, however, if you pay the premium. Thus, for the price of reimbursing your employer for the cost of your coverage, you could essentially *increase* your benefits by the net marginal savings from your taxes. You should therefore seriously consider offering to reimburse your employer for the cost of your disability coverage in order to receive the benefits tax-free, assuming you have not done so already.

In any event, if you are not eligible for Social Security Disability benefits, you should attempt to reenter the job market if at all possible.[22] If you later were to become disabled within the meaning of the Social Security statute, your eligibility for disability benefits would still depend on whether you were "fully insured," which is essentially a measure of whether you have worked long enough and recently enough to be entitled to benefits. If there is a significant gap between the time you quit working and the time you become sufficiently disabled to qualify for Social Security, you may discover that your eligibility for Social Security (and Medicare) benefits has lapsed.

---

[22] Although it certainly is not common, some employers (notably some temporary agencies) offer health insurance coverage to part-time employees.

Moreover, the longer you stay out of the job market, the more likely you are to not qualify for Social Security retirement benefits later. Without some form of Social Security eligibility, you also do not automatically qualify for Medicare, which is the only form of primary health insurance available to most retirees.[23]

You may use the Disability Needs Estimator worksheet following this section to assist you in determining how much monthly after-tax income you should insure against disability.

- **Summary of Present Coverage:** Record your total monthly disability benefits (column F of Disability Insurance Spreadsheet), but only include policies with a definition of disability based on your own occupation (see columns L and M). If a policy's definition of disability is based on your ability to work in *any* job, this is parallel to the Social Security standard of disability. If you fail to qualify for Social Security, it is likely your claim of disability would also be rejected by the insurance company under its policy. Additionally, consider the length of the policy coverage under each disability policy, and evaluate whether any gaps exist between your disability income provisions and your Social Security retirement age. If any income, qualification, or policy length gaps exist, make note of the specific gaps or amount of your shortfall in **Gaps in Coverage** and in your **Action Plan.** If your disability coverage exceeds your needs, note the amount of the excess in **Duplicate Coverage** and in your **Action Plan.** (Even if this is the case, you may want to consider whether you would have difficulty obtaining additional disability coverage in the future due to a medical condition or history. If that would be the case, it might make sense to overinsure now in order to have sufficient coverage if your needs were to increase in the future.)

[23] If you do not qualify for Social Security at retirement age, you have the option to pay the premiums yourself and buy into the system. However, before retirement age, if you do not qualify for Social Security benefits, you cannot obtain Medicare benefits.

Disability Needs Estimator

Part 1 Enter monthly expenses related to each of these items and add them. If possible, average what you spent during the last 6 months.

Mortgage or Rent	________
Utilities	________
Food	________
Auto/Transportation	________
Tuition/education expenses	________
Clothing	________
Loans and Installments	________
Insurance Premiums	________
Medical/Dental care costs	________
Miscellaneous expenses	________
Other Items not listed, including savings and investments.	________
Taxes	________
Subtotal	________

Part 2 Enter your monthly *AFTER TAX* income provided by each of the following sources of nonearned income. For the insurance items, check each policy's maximum benefits. For the other items, use a 6-month historical average, if available.

Group Disability Coverage	________
Other Insurance Benefits	________
Interest Income	________
Dividends	________
Rental Income	________
Residuals, Royalties, etc.	________
Subtotal	________

Subtract Part 2 Subtotal from Part 1 Subtotal. This is the amount of monthly income that you need to insure against disability.

Subtotal Part 1	________
Subtotal Part 2	________
Monthly Income To Insure	________

Category 4: Income Loss Due to Chronic Illness After 6 Months of Disability If Eligible for SSDI

Like the previous category, this one requires you to consider income replacement through disability insurance; this category allows you to include disability income you would obtain from Social Security Disability as well. You should ask yourself the same questions you considered in the prior category.

If you are eligible for Social Security Disability Insurance, you will not have to worry about qualifying for Medicare. However, as discussed later, you will not obtain Medicare for at least 29 months after you apply for your SSDI benefits, so again you should consider continued health benefits during this period. If you currently have employer-sponsored health insurance and you apply for Social Security immediately upon leaving employment, you will be entitled to 29 months of federally mandated continuation coverage through your employer's group (with you paying the premiums). After qualifying for Medicare you will still need to find ways to fill the health insurance gaps left by Medicare. In some states you may obtain Medigap coverage even before retirement age, but other states only provide Medigap plans for early retirees.[24] Thus, your income calculations for this period (and therefore the amount of disability insurance you will need) should take explicit account of how you will insure or pay for your health risks both before and after Medicare qualification. At a minimum, you might consider carrying an additional private catastrophic medical policy. For this category, if your future disability is predictable, you may want to consider using Credit Life and Disability Insurance to stretch your cash resources (see discussion under Action Plan later).

- **Summary of Present Coverage:** Record your total monthly disability benefits (column D of Disability Insurance Spreadsheet), net of offsets (column E of Disability Insurance Spreadsheet). Additionally, consider the length of the policy coverage under each disability policy, and evaluate whether any gaps exist between your disability income provisions and your Social Security retirement age. If a cessation event could occur before your Social Security retirement age (column N) or if the benefits provide an income gap, make note of the specific gaps or amount of your shortfall in **Gaps in Coverage** and in your **Action Plan.** If your disability coverage exceeds your needs, note the amount of the excess in **Duplicate Coverage** and in your **Action Plan.** (Again, you might want to consider future uninsurability and increased future needs as a reason to keep any extra coverage.)

Category 5: Income Loss During Subsequent Periods If Disability Policy Has Further Definition of Disability

This category requires you to consider disability income sources only if your policy has a "subsequent period" disability definition based on Social Security standards ("any job"). Even if you meet the disability standards for Social Security Disability, again you need to consider the sufficiency of disability income provided by your benefits after taxes.

"Subsequent Periods" refers to the provisions in your private disability policies. Many disability plans use one definition of disability for a particular

[24] See chart in Appendix 2 for a state-by-state comparison.

time (usually two years) and then adopt the more stringent Social Security definition for periods of disability following that time period. If your insurance plan does something similar, you will need to be prepared for the possibility of not qualifying for continuing disability payments if you also do not qualify for Social Security Disability.

If your disability policies have no changing disability definition feature and your coverage is otherwise adequate, you may disregard this risk factor.

- **Summary of Present Coverage:** Record your total monthly disability benefits (column D of Disability Insurance Spreadsheet), net of offsets (column E of Disability Insurance Spreadsheet). Then subtract any benefits from policies with "subsequent period" qualification definitions. Additionally, consider the length of the policy coverage under each disability policy and evaluate whether any gaps exist between your disability income provisions and your Social Security retirement age. If a cessation event could occur before your Social Security retirement age (column N) or if the benefits provide an income gap, make note of the specific gaps or amount of your shortfall in **Gaps in Coverage** and in your **Action Plan.** If your disability coverage exceeds your needs, note the amount of the excess in **Duplicate Coverage** and in your **Action Plan.** (Again, you might want to consider future uninsurability and increased future needs as a reason to keep any extra coverage.)

Categories 6 and 9: Income Loss to Dependents Following Death

This category requires you to consider whether you and your spouse have an adequate amount of life insurance and whether the form of the insurance meets your needs. The amount of life insurance you (or your spouse) should have can be estimated using an estimator worksheet, which allows an estimate to be made on the basis of your individual family circumstances and desires. For married couples, a separate worksheet should be prepared for each spouse.

The same considerations for the person with a chronic illness or disability should apply equally well for the spouse. Even if the spouse is not employed, if that spouse becomes a primary caretaker and thereafter dies, his or her services would have to be substituted by paid assistance, which demands some form of additional income or insurance coverage, or both.

In addition to considering whether you have adequate death benefits, you should consider the *form* of the life insurance (e.g., term life or whole life). Only whole life accrues cash values that can be used during your lifetime, whereas term life policies are less expensive. Generally, you should obtain whole life when you want certainty, if you will use your insurance for its cash values during your lifetime, or if you need the insurance to continue in force beyond the typical cessation of coverage of a term policy (well into old age).

To get a reasonably unbiased analysis of cash-value life insurance policies you may have or are considering purchasing, contact the Consumer Federation of America (CFA). This organization will evaluate any proposal you may receive as well as any policy you currently own (telephone 202-387-0087).[25]

---

[25] A fee may be required for this service.

- **Summary of Present Coverage:** After you have completed the estimator worksheet and determined your cash requirements, subtract available assets from total funds needed to cover expenses. Any shortfall represents the estimated amount of additional life insurance that is needed for your current portfolio. If there is a shortfall, obtaining the additional insurance should be noted in **Gaps in Coverage** and added to your **Action Plan.** Similarly, any excess insurance should be listed in **Duplicate Coverage** and added to your **Action Plan.** In preparing the estimator worksheet, you should also consider whether the family has comprehensive and continuous health, disability, and long-term care insurance, because without such insurance, health, disability, or long-term care costs will have to be paid directly out of the family budget (and should be added in the estimator). Finally, if you would like to include any of the "additional uses," you need to consider whether your insurance should be term or whole life. If you need to convert term life to whole life, you should make a note of this in your **Action Plan.** (Again, as with disability coverage, you may want to keep excess insurance you have now if you will have uninsurability issues in the future as your needs increase.

Comprehensive Life Insurance Estimator

Insured Name:
Age of Insured:
Age of Insured's Spouse:
Age(s) of Insured's Children:

Date:
Page 1

Expenses		Estimated Amounts	
1. Final expenses (one-time expenses incurred by death)	a. Final illness (medical costs will probably exceed health insurance deductibles and coinsurance, so assume that at least those amounts will have to be funded)	______	
	b. Burial/funeral costs	______	
	c. Probate costs (if unsure, assume 4% of assets passing through probate process)	______	
	d. Federal estate taxes (generally for estates over $1,000,000, but if estate is willed to spouse, no taxes may be due)*	______	
	e. State inheritance taxes (varies by state)*	______	
	f. Legal fees, estate administration	______	
	g. Other	______	
		Total Final Expenses	______
2. Outstanding debt (to be paid off at death)	a. Credit card/consumer debt	______	
	b. Automobile	______	
	c. Mortgage (if the family is to pay off the mortgage; otherwise, include mortgage payments in life income	______	

*For precise information, contact a qualified Estate Planning Attorney in your state.

d. Other ____________

Total Outstanding Debt ____________

3. Readjustment expenses (to cover transition period of immediate crisis)
   a. Child Care ____________
   b. Additional Homemaking Help ____________
   c. Vocational counseling/educational training (for a nonworking or under-employed spouse who expects to seek paid employment) ____________
   d. Other ____________

Total Readjustment Expenses ____________

4. Dependent expenses (untill all children are self-supporting) except school tuition
   a. Estimate of household annual expenses ____________
   b. To remove the deceased's personal expenses, multiply the figure in a. by: ** ____________
      0.70 for a surviving family of one
      0.74 for a surviving family of two
      0.78 for a surviving family of three
      0.80 for a surviving family of four
      0.82 for a surviving family of five
   c. Deduct spouse's estimated annual net after-tax income from employment ____________

Total Current Annual Expenses to be Covered ____________

**If the deceased person had significant expenses out of the ordinary, this should be reflected in the adjustment percentage.

Comprehensive Life Insurance Estimator (*Continued*)

Insured Name:
Age of Insured:

Date:
Page 3

Expenses		Estimated Amounts	
	d. Total Dependent Support: multiply number of years until youngest child becomes self-supporting by Total Above: multiply number of years support is expected to continue for dependent parents by Total Above:	***Total Dependent Expenses***	______
5. Education Expenses	a. Annual School Tuition	______	
	b. Multiply by number of years and children	______	
	c. Annual college costs in current dollars	______	
	d. Multiply by number of years and children	______	
		Total Educational Expenses	______ ***
6. Life Income for Surviving Spouse (after all children are self-supporting)	a. Annual Income desired (current dollars)	______	
	b. Deduct income from spouse's employment	______	
		Total Current Annual Dependent Expenses to be Covered	______
	c. Multiply by number of years between year last child becomes self-supporting and year when spouse begins receiving retirement income	______	
		Total Pre-Retirement Annual Expenses to be Covered	______

***Adjust this amount by any pre-paid or dedicated tuition plans already funded that will reduce overall costs.

7. Retirement Income for Surviving Spouse

a. Annual Income desired (current dollars) ____________________

b. Less Social Security and pension income ____________________

c. Multiply by life expectancy after retirement ____________________

Total Post-Retirement Annual Expenses to be Covered ____________________

Total Spouse Life Income Requirement (add together above totals in column E for pre- and post-retirement) ____________________

5. Total Additional Uses for Life Insurance (these amounts should be insurance accruing cash values)

a. Net value of estate to be shielded from spenddown if Medicaid is used to pay long-term care costs ____________________ (this amount must only be in the form of non-term insurance death benefit)

b. Additional amounts (if any) if used as a mortgage insurance substitute ____________________

c. Additional amounts to be used for long-term care through viatical or living benefit or loans against cash values. ____________________

d. Additional amounts for other uses (including possible direct finance of some long term care through loans against accrued cash values, paying estate taxes, or providing a sizeable charitable bequest) ____________________

Total Additional Non-Term Insurance ____________________

Comprehensive Life Insurance Estimator (*Continued*)

Insured Name: Date:
Age of Insured: Page 5

Expenses	Estimated Amounts	
6. Total Funds Needed to Cover Expenses	***Total Final Expenses***	
	Total Outstanding Debt	________
	Total Readjustment Expenses	________
	Total Dependent Expenses	________
	Total Education Expenses	________
	Total Spouse Life Income Requirement	________
	Total Additional Non-Term Insurance	________
	Grand Total of Funds Needed	________

Assets Available to Support Family

a. Proceeds from current life insurance ________

b. Cash and savings ________

c. Equity in real estate (if to be sold) ________

d. Securities ________

e. IRA, Keogh plans, Lump-sum pensions ________

f. Employer savings plans & other sources ________

Total Available Assets ________

Total Additional Non-Term Insurance

a. Paid-Up Whole Life Insurance ______________

b. Paid-Up Universal Life Insurance ______________

c. Paid-Up Other Life Insurance ______________

Total Paid-Up Non-Term Life Insurance ______________

Category 7: Income Loss or Need for Additional Income Due To Disability of Spouse

As with life insurance, even a nonworking spouse of a person with a chronic illness or disability should consider the need for disability insurance. As noted earlier, if the spouse becomes a primary caretaker and thereafter becomes disabled, the spouse's services would have to be substituted by paid assistance, which demands some form of additional income.* Also, if the primary breadwinner becomes so disabled that he or she must discontinue employment, it may be necessary for the spouse to find a job to create family income. If that occurs and the well spouse then becomes disabled, the couple would need income replacement for the lost wages of the well spouse. Nor should you wait any length of time to secure adequate disability insurance because it is impossible to predict when a health condition will occur that will make it difficult to obtain good coverage.

- **Summary of Present Coverage:** Record your spouse's total monthly disability benefits (column D of Disability Insurance Spreadsheet), net of offsets (column E of Disability Insurance Spreadsheet). Then subtract any benefits from policies with "subsequent period" qualification definitions. Additionally, consider the length of the policy coverage under each disability policy and evaluate whether any gaps exist between your spouse's disability income provisions and his or her Social Security retirement age. If a cessation event could occur before your spouse's Social Security retirement age (column N) or if the benefits provide an income gap, make note of the specific gaps or amount of your spouse's shortfall in **Gaps in Coverage** and in your spouse's **Action Plan.** If your spouse's disability coverage exceeds his or her needs, note the amount of the excess in **Duplicate Coverage** and in your spouse's **Action Plan.**

Category 8: Income Loss Due to Unemployment of the Spouse of Person With Chronic Illness or Disability

If your spouse needs to return to work to make up an income shortfall between your household's monthly income needs and what your disability insurance actually provides, you will need to make sure that the income stream continues even in the event of his or her unemployment. This requires you to determine how much income your spouse actually needs to produce to meet monthly expenses and how many months of expenses your own personal savings can provide during unemployment. As a general rule of thumb, you should have at least six months of savings available for this purpose *after* you have used your savings during elimination periods and established eligibility for Social Security or other disability income sources.

- **Summary of Present Coverage:** Note in this category whether your current personal savings are adequate to sustain you through your original elimination periods as well as six more months of spouse unemployment (the latter measured by the amount of income that needs to be contributed by the spouse based on disability income shortfalls). If not, make note of the amount of your shortfall in your **Gaps in Coverage** and in your **Action Plan.**

---

*It will probably be difficult to find traditional insurance for a spouse who can demonstrate no earnings. At a minimum the family should nevertheless make some arrangement to augment cash resources if the caretaking spouse becomes incapacitated.

Category 9: Spouse Life Insurance

See discussion under Category 6.

Categories 10 & 11: Risk of Inflation During Periods of Disability

The risk of inflation demands that whatever disability products you obtain have some mechanism built into them to adjust for inflation. Without such a mechanism, you and your spouse will be subject to a constant degradation of the value of all disability benefits relative to the cost of living. This is particularly critical for a person facing disability at a fairly young age.

- **Summary of Present Coverage:** Check column E of the disability insurance spreadsheets for both you and your spouse to see if you have an inflation benefit. In addition, check the worksheet to see exactly what that benefit is. If you think it is sufficient, you do not need to do anything. If you need better coverage, note this in **Gaps in Coverage** and add to your **Action Plan.**

Category 12: Health Expenses for Chronic Illness/Disability After Diagnosis and During Employment

This category requires you to evaluate your health insurance coverage for your chronic illness or disability while you are still employed. Chances are that if your employer sponsors health insurance, that is what you rely on to cover your expenses. Beware! Even though most financial planners prefer employment-based health insurance because of its financial or tax advantages, a strong word of caution about employment-based health or other insurance is in order. It may be cheaper or tax advantaged, but it is most definitely *not* better.

Most Americans with group major medical and hospital insurance get their insurance through their employers. This "employer-based" group health insurance often carries some significant risks and pitfalls of which most people are not aware. Given some of the problems that you may encounter if you become ill, you may be better off spending more money now to get group or individual health insurance that is not based on employment, even if you do not currently have a disability.

If your insurance is based on your *own* employment, the onset of your own disability may become the very event that causes you to lose your insurance. Employer-based group health insurance is usually available only in two cases. Either the insurance will have a class of eligible people that includes you (e.g., "employee" or someone connected to an employee, such as a spouse) or you qualify for "COBRA" continuation benefits as defined by federal law. Most primary eligible participants are limited to current, full-time, active employees. Only a few employers include retired employees as an eligible class. If your employer does not include part-time or disability-retired employees as an eligible class, you would be required to forfeit your group health benefits if you become sick enough that you must leave full-time work. You would then only be entitled to what federal law mandates through COBRA coverage. COBRA coverage, even for someone who has left work due to disability and who applies for Social Security, only extends for a maximum of 29 months (18 months in most other cases). At the end of the COBRA period, you would need to get insurance from the private marketplace or another source. Even if your employer includes disability-retired employees as an eligible class, your employer may still not be prevented from eliminating or degrading benefits to that class at some future date in order to cut costs. The bottom line is that as long as your health insurance is based on someone's employment, it is not as bulletproof as it should be to guarantee peace of mind.

This system of employer-based private insurance has enabled the private insurance marketplace to keep costs down, at least in part, by shifting many of the high-cost users out of commercially available insurance risk pools. Of course, another possible way to keep costs down is for the carrier to refuse to pay legitimate claims. The legal structure of employer-based policies actually *encourages* more recalcitrance in employer-based groups than in other forms of health insurance groups. This is because employer-based plans are protected from state litigation by federal preemption established in a law known as "ERISA" (Employee Retirement Income Security Act). Thus, even remedies that your state legislature has established for recalcitrant insurers will not be available for you to apply against your employer's insurer.

Additionally, employer-sponsored insurance is inadequate in most cases because it is not guaranteed to continue until you qualify for Medicare and Medigap insurance during disability or retirement. Should you change jobs, you also have no guarantee that you can replace the coverage from your prior employer with equally comprehensive coverage for a reasonable premium. While federal law does mandate that you be given the option of obtaining a private policy from an insurer after your COBRA benefits expire after leaving employment, the law neither mandates the content of that "conversion" policy nor limits the premium payments on such policies.

Bottom line: Run—do not walk—to your closest professional, trade, alumni, or other association to find out what kinds of group major medical or hospital plans are available to you. The sooner you have coverage that depends upon *membership* instead of *employment*, the better your remedies and disability-retention rights will be if and when you really need your insurance to perform. Of course, the longer you wait, the more likely it is that you will acquire a disqualifying health condition that will make it much more difficult to obtain good coverage. Even if you think you cannot afford an additional primary health insurance policy, you may be able to obtain group catastrophic or "excess" major medical coverage for a very modest premium. (See discussion about catastrophic insurance later.)

Another important issue to consider is how you will fund health expenses for conditions other than the chronic illness or disability. This is often the most overlooked component of insurance in a family with a chronically ill or disabled member. Just because a member of a family has a chronic illness or disability (and therefore may not be able to obtain optimal health coverage for that illness or disability), this does not require that all other health needs for the entire family should be subjected to the lowest common denominator of coverage available for the chronic illness or disability. One good way to deal with other health needs is to take a "waiver" or exclusion for the chronic illness or disability in an otherwise good insurance policy. In that way, it may be possible to obtain good, thorough, long-term coverage for the person with the chronic illness or disability (*sans* the chronic medical condition), along with good overall coverage for other members of the family. This strategy requires you to be willing to pay for more than one health policy, but the improvement in coverage should make the additional investment worthwhile.

Thus, it makes more sense to *segregate* your health coverage needs and seek out one good, portable, non–employment-based major medical (and hospitalization) policy for all health risks *except* the chronic illness or disability (these are often called policies with "waiver" or "exclusion" provisions). Then the only risks left to insure would include the risks attributable to the chronic illness or disability, and these should be separately insured.

- **Summary of Present Coverage:** Review your health insurance spreadsheet and determine whether you have at least one good comprehensive policy (based on part B worksheet evaluations) that is not based on continued employment of yourself or your spouse and that covers your diagnosed chronic illness or disability. If your employer provides a contractual guarantee of continued group health coverage indefinitely after disability and into retirement, you may consider that insurance as well.[26] If you do not have such a policy, note this fact in **Gaps in Coverage** and in your **Action Plan.** If you have (and are paying for more than one such policy), you may be able to reduce premiums by letting one policy lapse. If this is the case, note that fact in **Duplicate Coverage** and in your **Action Plan.** NOTE: With typical major medical and hospitalization policies, there is a provision in the policy called "Coordination of Benefits" that prevents you from recovering your expenses twice. This is *not* true of most hospital indemnity type health policies, in which case you can collect under more than one policy under appropriate circumstances (see discussion below about hospital indemnity plans).

Category 13: Health Expenses After Employment Ceases Due to Disability If SSDI Eligible

This category challenges you to consider how you will cover continuing medical expenses after you leave employment. Except in the rare circumstance in which an employer contractually promises indefinitely to continue group health benefits during disability or into retirement, cessation of employment due to disability is almost always followed by the inevitable consequence of the loss of health insurance benefits. Federal law mandates that you be given an opportunity to obtain continuation coverage for your employer-sponsored health benefits, but the law only requires that those benefits be provided for 18 months under most circumstance or 29 months if you apply for SSDI. Even if you qualify for Social Security Disability, you will have to endure at least 29 months following application for SSDI before you will be eligible for Medicare. Even if your employment COBRA health benefits extend long enough to get you to Medicare eligibility, you will soon discover that Medicare by itself is an inferior and unpre-

---

[26] In relying on the contractual guarantee, you should be aware that you are relying on the financial stability of the employer to the same extent that you are relying on the financial strength of the insurer. Additionally, you will be betting on your own continued employment by the employer for a long period of time, coupled with the presumption that you would not, in any event, become sick or disabled, and therefore difficult to insure, before you could be laid off. These assumptions do not adhere to the principle of planning for the worst. For these reasons, I think it is a mistake to rely on these guarantees for continued health coverage. I nevertheless mention the option because to most people it seems so alluring.

dictable form of health coverage. If you happen to be lucky enough to live in a state where you may obtain supplemental Medigap insurance as a nonelderly adult,[27] you are in luck. If you are not, you will have to do some serious planning NOW, before this issue of lack of reasonable health coverage ever arises.

Financial plans must assume long-term, predictable strategies. For this reason, government benefits such as Medicare, while not irrelevant, should be used as planning tools only as a last resort. Government benefits are too unreliable and difficult to predict and enforce to serve as good planning tools. Guaranteed continuous, private insurance contracts with identifiable rights and obligations and with good state enforcement remedies are far superior tools. While that does not mean that you should ignore the availability of government benefits such as Medicare in devising a protection portfolio,[28] those benefits should generally not serve as anything other than *second-line* or alternative strategies. You should instead—if possible—devise a plan with private resources, falling back on government resources only as a last resort if your own good planning cannot ameliorate all of the areas of risk you had to assume.

- **Summary of Present Coverage:** Based on your health insurance spreadsheet, determine whether you have either (1) employer-sponsored health coverage with a contractual guarantee from the employer for continued coverage during disability; or (2) other good health insurance coverage including coverage for the chronic illness or disability (see content evaluation from worksheet part B); or (3) you live in a state where good Medigap coverage is available to supplement Medicare. If you do not meet these criteria, note this fact in **Gaps in Coverage** and your **Action Plan.** If you have duplicate health coverage, you may consider eliminating one plan (keep a private plan in addition to Medicare, however) and note this in **Duplicate Coverage** and your **Action Plan.**

Category 14: Health Expenses After Employment Ceases Due to Disability If Not SSDI Eligible

This category requires you to consider how you will cover your health expenses after you leave employment if you will not ultimately qualify for SSDI (and therefore will not be eligible for Medicare or Medigap insurance). The principles discussed in Category 13 apply equally well here.

- **Summary of Present Coverage:** Based on your health insurance spreadsheet, determine whether you have either (1) employer-sponsored health coverage with a contractual guarantee from the employer for continued coverage during disability; or (2) other good health insurance coverage including coverage for the chronic illness or disability (see content evaluation from worksheet part B). If you do not meet these criteria, note this fact in **Gaps in Coverage** and your **Action Plan.** If you have duplicate health coverage, you may consider eliminating one plan and note this in **Duplicate Coverage** and your **Action Plan.**

---

[27] Contact your state insurance commissioner for information about Medigap coverage in your state. For a list of contact information for state insurance regulators, see Appendix 1.

[28] For example, a common problem overlooked in estate plans is the effect inheritances or gifts may have on eligibility for public benefits such as Medicaid. In certain circumstances, it may be preferable to limit or eliminate the transfer of assets so that the beneficiary is not put in the position of missing out on valuable social services such as long-term care for which insurance may be unavailable due to a health condition or age.

Category 15: Health Expenses After Retirement If You Are Eligible for Social Security Retirement Benefits

This category requires you to consider what kind of health insurance coverage you will have after you retire. The toughest health insurance nut to crack is post-retirement insurance. Most health plans (except for employer plans for current employees) only cover people until age 65.[29] A few employer plans also cover retirees. Even those plans, if offered as a benefit to the employees and not as a matter of contract, can be changed by the employer to reduce costs. In reality, most people above retirement age rely on Medicare and Medigap insurance for their coverage. For this reason it is critical that a person with a chronic illness or disability remain "fully insured" under the Social Security laws. This can be done either by drawing disability or by working. It is *not* advisable for a person with a chronic illness or disability to leave the work force without qualifying for Social Security. Even if your insurance is sufficient today, it may not be available when you reach retirement age. For that reason you need to be careful to check the cessation events you listed in your health insurance spreadsheet in order to plan for continued coverage even throughout retirement.

- **Summary of Present Coverage:** Based on your health insurance spreadsheet, determine whether you have either (1) employer-sponsored health coverage with a contractual guarantee from the employer for continued coverage during disability until Social Security retirement age or through retirement; or (2) other good health insurance coverage including coverage for the chronic illness or disability (see content evaluation from worksheet part B) until Social Security retirement age; and (3) eligibility for Social Security (and Medicare) upon retirement. If you do not meet these criteria, note this fact in **Gaps in Coverage** and your **Action Plan.** This is especially true if there is a gap between your insurance cessation event (usually based on age) and the age at which you would otherwise become eligible for Social Security. If you have duplicate health coverage, you may consider eliminating one plan and note this in **Duplicate Coverage** and your **Action Plan.**

Category 16: Health Expenses After Retirement If You Are Neither Social Security Retirement Nor Medicaid Eligible

This category requires you to consider how you will cover your health expenses after retirement if you are not eligible for Social Security Retirement (and therefore are not automatically eligible for Medicare) and also are not automatically eligible for Medicaid (the federal poverty health plan). Fortunately, Medicare allows elderly people who are not automatically eligible for Medicare to buy-in to the Medicare system to obtain Medicare coverage. As an elderly Medicare recipient, you can supplement Medicare with Medigap insurance.

- **Summary of Present Coverage:** Based on your health insurance spreadsheet, determine whether you have either (1) employer-sponsored health coverage with a contractual guarantee from the employer for continued coverage

[29] For people whose Social Security retirement age is later than age 65, even this kind of provision in a pre-retirement policy will create a gap in coverage if coverage is not available between age 65 and your actual full-eligibility Social Security retirement age. See Appendix 4.

during disability until Social Security retirement age, or through retirement; or (2) other good health insurance coverage including coverage for the chronic illness or disability (see content evaluation from worksheet part B) until Social Security retirement age. If not, then you will need to buy-in to Medicare to obtain coverage. If you do not meet these criteria, note this fact in **Gaps in Coverage** and your **Action Plan.** This is especially true if there is a gap between your insurance cessation event (usually based on age) and the age at which you would otherwise become eligible for Social Security. If you have duplicate health coverage, you may consider eliminating one plan and note this in **Duplicate Coverage** and your **Action Plan.**

Category 17: Long-Term Care If Your Family Cannot Provide Care

Very few people have purchased long-term care insurance. Part of the reason for this undoubtedly is that most people do not really have a clear understanding of what comprises long-term care until they need it. In part that is because the concept has changed so much over recent years.

A 1996 survey conducted by the National Council on Aging concluded that most people still believe that "long-term care" is a euphemism for "custodial care" in a nursing home. That study showed that approximately 50 percent of the respondents had either no or little awareness of other services included within the rubric of "long-term care."

In fact, long-term care includes a wide range of medical and personal assistance for people who, for whatever reason, are not able to provide for their own needs. Traditionally, the choices for such care were limited to: (1) care at home from a spouse; (2) care from adult children; or (3) care in a nursing home. Today other options have been developed to preserve an individual's personal autonomy and dignity and to allow people to stay in their own environment. These services can loosely be categorized in three ways: (1) nursing home care; (2) home and community-based care (including home health care, homemaker/chore service, emergency response systems, and adult day care); and (3) respite care.

If long-term care does become necessary and is beyond the ability of your own family to provide for at little or no cost,[30] try to determine which services or facilities might be at least partially covered by government programs or private insurance and which are available at low or no cost. If you have a good, comprehensive, long-term care policy (and one for your spouse), you are in a good position. Because Medicare only provides very limited long-term care benefits,[31] if you do not have adequate insurance to cover the costs of needed care and you still cannot obtain the resources necessary to pay for long-term care from your own resources, your only realistic available option may be to

---

[30] There are many steps that you can take now to reduce your need for assistance later, such as securing a wheelchair-friendly home on accessible municipal transportation lines. Your overall life circumstances will determine—to a great extent—both the type and availability of assistance you will need at a later date. If you find inadequate resources for long-term services, you should begin now (while you are relatively healthy) to restructure your life circumstances to reduce your *need* for care later.

[31] For example, nursing home benefits are limited to 100 days.

establish eligibility for Medicaid, the state health care program for low-income individuals. The amount of your income and assets, as well as your spouse's income and assets, may determine whether Medicaid will be able to provide care at home or only in a nursing facility. Each state has different rules, and you should consult your state Medicaid agency or an attorney specializing in Elder Law to determine what the restrictions are. You must be *very* careful when trying to make your income and assets low enough to qualify for Medicaid. Medicaid rules and varying state rules, severely restrict protective transfers of income and assets.[32]

If after determining what your income and assets are you determine that only Medicaid would fill the gap for you in paying for nursing care, you should start now by creating legal ownership of income and assets that would make the disabled person immediately eligible for Medicaid when the time comes that long-term care becomes necessary beyond the capacity of the family to provide.[33] This includes not only transferring assets in acceptable ways (taking into account the ineligibility period or transfer restrictions) but also structuring income sources so that the checks are drawn in the well-spouse's name. If at-home care is desired and the disabled spouse would not qualify for such care in any event under the state's income limitations, a last resort is to obtain a divorce that divides income and assets in such a way that the disabled spouse is left with transferable assets and no disqualifying income sources so as to qualify for Medicaid. In planning your finances for possible eligibility for Medicaid, you should consult with an elder law attorney. A reference to the National Academy of Elder Lawyers is listed in "Resources" at the end of this book.

[32] To understand how complex these issues are, it helps to understand the basic rules. Generally, for a spouse entering a nursing home, anything transferred from their name during the 30-month period before entering a nursing facility or applying for Medicaid is considered an invalid transfer and will delay eligibility for Medicaid. However, there are some exceptions to this 30-month rule, Medicaid allows an at-home spouse to retain some liquid assets and income, as well as allowing the couple to change the title on their home when one spouse enters a nursing facility. Other assets also may be exempt from these rules, such as a car and some personal belongings. Additionally, there are some people to whom you may transfer anything at any time, including a minor, blind, or disabled child. A spouse also may transfer any asset of his or her at-home spouse, but only if the at-home spouse does not transfer it to anyone else within 30 months, for less than its true value. You may also invest your liquid assets in the home by paying off an outstanding mortgage, making improvements, or buying a new home for more money than your present home is worth. Whatever you do, though, must result in a home that the at-home spouse actually lives in. Of course, an additional benefit of paying off any mortgage or increasing the value of the home is to make more equity available in case a reverse mortgage could be useful at a later time.

The more difficult issue is dealing with income sources. Assuming that you as the well spouse have enough independent income to survive, your spouse may be able to set up something called an income-cap trust (also known as a "Miller" trust) for income he or she receives above the Medicaid qualifying amount. The essential problem addressed here is that all of a spouse's income and assets are deemed to be available to the other spouse if they are living together (but not if divorced). However, if one spouse is in a nursing facility for more than a month, most states have income eligibility limits that use a "name-on-the-check" rule. Essentially, after the first month, if the income is received in the name of the at-home spouse, it is generally not counted toward the state's maximum income limit for the other spouse's Medicaid eligibility. Therefore, the only income that remains at issue after the first month is income received in the name of the spouse not at-home.

[33] In many states there are experts in estate planning for families with children who have disabilities. You can obtain current information for such experts in the September issue of Exceptional Parent magazine or by contacting the National Information Center for Children and Youth with Disabilities, P.O. Box 1492, Washington, DC 20013 (800) 999-5599.

You should also make sure that involved family members begin to think about their own financial contributions. Although there may be no immediate need for money from relatives, the decisions made about long-term care may determine when money from beyond your own resources will be required. The earlier the possibility is discussed, the easier it will be to plan and provide for it.

- **Summary of Present Coverage:** Consider whether you have a good long-term care policy (based on your long-term care policy evaluation). If not, and if after considering all resources you may have for raising private funds to pay for care directly, you may have to plan now for later Medicaid eligibility. If that is the case, note this in **Gaps in Coverage** and in your **Action Plan.** Do not forget to add an action item to evaluate all sources of cash to determine whether or how much long-term care you could personally finance.

Action Plan

In your evaluation worksheet, your **Action Plan** column should now summarize all of the steps you need to take to shore up your basic health, life, disability, and long-term care coverages. Your action plan should also disclose shortfalls you may have in income or savings now that may be required to develop the cash resources you will require for a disability that may occur later. This section is designed to assist you in your efforts to secure additional insurance coverage or to develop substitutes that can serve as insurance alternatives. This section also shows you how, in two instances, insurance products might be helpful in generating cash or other resources precisely *because* you become disabled.[34]

If you would like to scout for insurance price quotes on the individual insurance market in cyberspace, look up InsWeb, a consortium of insurance agents and carriers that combines health insurance information and links to agencies worldwide. InsWeb can be found at: http://www.insweb.com/. Other web resources are listed in "Resources" at the end of this book.

■ DISABILITY INSURANCE

As with **group**[35] term life and health benefits, it is possible to obtain disability insurance *even after diagnosis* through an association "guaranteed issue" plan.[36]

---

[34] See discussions below about credit life & disability insurance and hospital indemnity insurance.

[35] It is important to distinguish between individual insurance—which is underwritten, if at all, based upon the risks presented by the *individual* being insured, and **group** insurance, in which the characteristics of the group as a whole are considered for underwriting. The larger the group is, the less that the characteristics of a single individual will alter the risks for the whole group; thus, the less that a pre-existing condition matters! When the group is large enough to overcome the risks presented by a single individual, the insurance may be offered on a "guaranteed issue" basis—meaning that it will be sold to all comers regardless of risk.

[36] Association group insurance is explained on an Internet web site at http://www.aafp.org/family/aafpins/monograp.html

In order to find these plans, you must become a sleuth in finding associations that offer them. There are no guarantees that everybody will be able to identify a nonemployer group they may join that will offer them such coverage. Your local library may have a reference book called *The Encyclopedia of Associations* that has a long list of potential sources for group coverage. Trying to find insurance with this tool would certainly seem daunting. The Internet makes such a challenge much more manageable. If you do not have Internet access at home or work, you may be able to obtain access at your local public library.

One basic principle to understand is that you need not necessarily "fit" the membership target for the association in order to join. For example, you are perfectly free to join the National Association for the Self-Employed, even if you aren't.[37] Or, if you happen to be a professional, you may be free to join the association of a *different* profession or trade, as long as some professional or trade certification you do not have is prerequisite to joining. Nor should you be leery of paying membership dues (as long as you get adequate insurance value for it). Financially, you should just consider the dues to be an additional insurance premium for that policy when you calculate the relative value of the insurance purchased.

In order to begin your search, you need to sign on to the Internet. If you are a graduate of a college or university, start by looking up your own alumni association's web site (use ".edu" as the extension). If you are a member of a church, try looking up their web site if they have one (use ".org" as the extension). Many churches are listed on http://churches.net. If you are a member of a professional or trade association (or could be), try looking up the association's web site if it has one. These are probably your best bets for association memberships offering group insurance. If you are not sure of the association's name, you may need to use a general search engine. If there is no web site or if the web site does not provide enough information, try to call the organization directly and ask the pertinent questions.

If you need to look further than the obvious potential associations you could join, you should use a search engine. A search of the word "association" may bring back in excess of one million listings. Consequently, a better strategy is to use the word "association" and some other identifier to narrow the search. For example, I am a lawyer and can find references to approximately 70,000 web listings when I search the term "law association." I could also search "law organization" or "law society" or a similar term to find additional references. Do not, however, make the mistake of researching "association insurance" because you will discover yourself wallowing around among web sites for insurance brokers and the like.

Imagination is your only limit. While researching the various sites, you should look for membership information or membership benefits. Then, specifically look to see if group insurance benefits are available. If extensive information is available online, look to see if the insurance is guaranteed issue and, if so, under what circumstances. If the information is not available, just bookmark the site and jot down the toll-free (or other) number for later calling if necessary. Of course, you should also see what the requirements and dues are for membership in the group to make sure you are not wasting your time.

As you are evaluating disability insurance, some questions you should ask include:

[37] http://selfemployed.nase.org/NASE

1. How much does it cost?

   The best way to lower the premium usually is to extend the initial waiting period before payment begins.

2. How long will benefits be paid?

   Consider especially whether the definition of disability changes at some point so that benefits may actually become disputed. Also look for a benefit period that will cover you until at least age 65, or older if your Social Security retirement age is raised. The age 65 cutoff presumes that Social Security will kick in at that point and provide you with an income. Thus, if your retirement is deferred by Social Security, you need to make sure your insurance contains coverage through that period.

3. What exactly are the benefits?

   Look for total disability benefits that replace at least 60 percent of your income after taxes. Are the benefits adjusted for inflation? With individual coverage, you can get a rider that provides a cost-of-living-adjustment. Are Social Security or Worker's Compensation or other income sources deducted?

4. How is income or salary defined?

   This is especially important for people who have a base salary that is increased through bonuses, consulting, or overtime.

5. What is the waiting period (the period you must wait before benefits begin)?

   You should not have a waiting period longer than your own personal savings can sustain you, including the possible increased costs due to medical bills or need for additional help at home. However, increasing the waiting period will substantially lower the premiums.

6. How is disability defined?

   Try to find a policy that provides coverage if you are unable to work in your *own occupation* or your *usual occupation*. Less advantageous is a policy that defines disability in terms of *inability to perform any occupation for which you are qualified by education or training*. Worst of all is a policy that defines disability as *inability to perform any occupation at all*.

7. Does the policy cover partial disability? If so, how?

   Without partial disability benefits, a policy won't pay anything unless you are completely incapable of working. You may be sick enough that you can't work full-time but can manage a reduced schedule. You may also be well enough to take a job, but not the demanding one you used to have and at lower pay. If such benefits are provided, does the policy only cover partial disability *after* you begin collecting benefits for *total* disability? In other words, is it possible within the terms of the policy to collect benefits if your disability forces you to work part-time, rather than not at all?

8. Are there excluded medical conditions, or merely a waiting period for coverage of certain medical conditions?

9. Is there a waiver of premium during disability?

   Look for a "waiver of premium" clause or rider explicitly within the policy.

10. Is the policy "noncancellable" or "guaranteed renewable?"

They may sound like the same thing, but they are not. Noncancellable policies have fixed premiums throughout the life of the contract. When you buy such a policy, you are assured that your premiums will never rise. With a guaranteed renewable policy, your insurer can raise premium rates if it does so for all group policies in a certain class. Group insurers have to petition state insurance departments for approval to do this, but if they can prove their claims are much higher than expected, they'll get the go-ahead. Ideally, you want a policy that cannot be cancelled.

■ CREDIT LIFE AND DISABILITY INSURANCE

You may find it difficult to obtain all the disability insurance you need to replace income sources you will lose if you quit working. Nevertheless, your disability may make it possible for you to generate financial resources from Credit Life & Disability Insurance if you carefully follow the terms of the policies and use advance planning to take advantage of these policies. Make sure you clearly understand *what* benefits you will receive and the *conditions* under which you may receive them *before* you consider using these policies.

Credit Life & Disability insurance is usually offered by creditors such as banks and credit card companies as a way of guaranteeing continuity of payments of your credit obligations even if your income is interrupted due to involuntary reasons. Most of these plans allow the consumer debtor to suspend payments during periods, for example, of disability or involuntary unemployment, and some policies even provide that the payments will be made *for* the debtor under certain circumstances.[38] In order for consumers to take advantage of these plans, it is important to read them *carefully* and to do advance planning before they are ever used.

At the outset, if you decide you want to implement a plan with this type of insurance, you should try to line up sources of credit that you can tap years later without incurring any substantial expenses just for having them in the meantime. Thus, credit cards with no annual fees are a good starting point, whereas credit cards or lines of credit with annual fees will cost you money even when you do not use them. You may wish to consider collecting a number of credit cards with no annual fees and just "file" them away for future

[38] In a nutshell, these plans are designed to make sure that the creditor gets paid even if the customer is incapable of continuing payments. The creditor's interest, therefore, is simply to make sure that its own profit is not interrupted, and it is not terribly concerned with whether the consumer benefits from the policies or not. The creditor (the bank or credit card company) may reinsure (*e.g.*, pass on its own exposure to another insurer) its own obligation to suspend or compensate for payments it foregoes under these plans, and thereby may pay a fixed premium to its reinsurer to make sure that it gets payment for its insured consumers even when the insured consumers cannot make the payments themselves. The Credit Life & Disability plans that are reinsured are therefore merely mirrors of the exposures that the creditors have themselves reinsured, and the creditors therefore do not "lose" money even when claims are filed under these plans, because the creditors are themselves insured against such loss with their own reinsurers; therefore they merely look to the reinsurer for income rather than to the consumer directly when the policy conditions for benefit payments are met. The premiums paid by the consumers to the creditor for this reinsured coverage more than cover the premiums paid by the creditor to its reinsurer, so these plans can also become a profit center for the creditor, instead of an insurance expense. This also explains why creditors market these plans with such rigor.

use.[39] If you plan to do this, you should also request copies of the Credit Life & Disability plans for each card to make sure you know what you will get when or if you eventually sign up for such insurance.[40] If the policy will not meet your needs, cancel the credit account to free up your credit rating (unless you need the card for other reasons).

When you evaluate Credit Life & Disability, you should pay close attention to several issues:

- Note the precise maximum *benefit*. If the benefit is mere *suspension* of payments (as compared to *payments made for you* in other plans, including *both principal and interest*), the actual benefit is really limited to the elimination of *interest* on any debt you may have, and not the actual debt itself. In other words, you are being forgiven the interest on the debt for a specified period of time you otherwise would have paid if the payments had continued uninterrupted. The principal balance remains to be paid off in the future despite the temporary suspension of payments.

  If you have credit balances when you become disabled, these types of policies may be useful in reducing your monthly expenses if you transfer balances to them within the requirements of the policies so that they are covered by the policy benefits. But, beware—this strategy only works for as long as the benefit period lasts. For example, Discover Card® AccountGuard℠ suspends payments only, and has a maximum benefit period of one year. Thus, the best benefit you could obtain with that credit card is a suspension of payments for one year (without incurring additional finance charges). Such a benefit could be useful, for example, during the pendency of a Social Security application or while waiting for other income to become available, and will thus stretch the limited resources you may have for a short time (and thus compensate for a lack of other cash resources during that time). However, this type of benefit will not help to *generate additional* resources, and in any event, is not a long-term solution to a cash shortfall. To generate resources using Credit Life & Disability, you need to acquire policies that will actually make principal and interest payments for you during benefit periods.[41]

---

[39] Be aware that the existence of such credit may—but will not necessarily—diminish your ability to secure further credit, even if the cards are never used. How such unusued credit will affect you depends upon the scoring of your credit report by each individual creditor.

[40] To the extent you are able to predict when your disability will begin, you become a good candidate for taking advantage of these types of plans. If possible, you should not sign up for them (and incur the expense for them) until you think you have a plan for using them. As a general rule, these types of benefits are *much* more expensive than traditional disability insurance, and it is usually more prudent to acquire savings and investments for times of trouble with the premiums you might otherwise pay for these plans. However, if you can *predict* disability in the future, you may be able to take good advantage of these plans as sources for additional resources during that disability, so long as you have taken into account the need to sign up in advance of any required waiting period and complied with the other conditions of the policies. In this way, you can minimize the number of months you pay premiums before you begin collecting benefits.

[41] If you can acquire debt before a benefit period that will be paid off for you during a benefit period, the amount of that debt effectively becomes an additional "resource." It may not be straight cash for you to spend, but the resource is just as valuable as cash because it *replaces* the *need* for cash that would otherwise have been used to acquire the resources the debt was used to finance. With such additional resources, Credit Life & Disability plans may help you with some cash shortfalls during periods of disability. Pay close attention to the terms and conditions of your plans to make sure you understand exactly what debt is covered by the plan benefit, and precisely what that benefit will accomplish for you and for how long.

- Take account of the precise circumstances under which the benefit is available, including the definitions of such circumstances, and any exclusionary or limiting clauses.

  For example, Discover Card® AccountGuard℠ covers a number of circumstances, including involuntary unemployment, disability due to accident or illness, and unpaid-employer-approved leave of absences. Under this plan, "disability" is defined under that same plan as "an accident or illness that prevents you from performing the material and substantial duties of your job or, if you are retired or are otherwise unemployed, that would prevent you from performing the material and substantial duties of any and all jobs." Among the further exclusions is a limited pre-existing clause: you do not qualify for benefits due to "disability during the first six months of Discover AccountGuard coverage arising from an accident or illness that caused you to consult with a physician or seek medical treatment within 6 months prior to enrolling for Discover AccountGuard." These definitions are significant. First, disability is not defined as the presence or absence of any known medical condition. It is instead specifically tied to *employment* and *performance of a job or jobs*. Thus, as long as a person with a known medical condition is employed, she is not considered "disabled" within the meaning of this policy, and her potential to collect benefits is equal to that of healthy members of the general public after six months! If she is working, and takes out the insurance at least 6 months before leaving employment due to disability, then she would be eligible for benefits *even if she were receiving significant medical treatment when she signed up for benefits and could anticipate some future disability at that time*. In essence, this policy could be used by a person with a disability who was planning eventual cessation of employment due to disability and subsequent application for Social Security. If that person has credit obligations that could be transferred to this card, that person could suspend payments for up to one year, and thus reduce income requirements (and preserve credit history) while waiting for Social Security benefits to begin. In sum, the policy definitions of these types of plans may lend themselves to some forms of risk planning for disability, even if you have a known condition, as long as you are actively working.

■ LIFE INSURANCE

If, after finishing the estimator, you discover that you need more life insurance but cannot seem to locate it through traditional means, you will have to become more creative. There are actually several options, in addition to trying to buy extra coverage through your employer.[42]

Convert Existing Term Policies

You might want to start converting some of your existing individual term life policies to whole life if you need more cash value-accruing or lifelong insurance. Don't be afraid to try to convert your individual policies on your own, even if that is not explicitly offered in the policy.

[42] Life insurance in excess of $55,000 per year provided by an employer will result in a *taxable* employee benefit (with taxes paid on the additional premium paid for benefits over $55,000).

Obtain as Many Group Memberships as Possible with "Guaranteed Issue" Group Life Insurance

As with disability insurance, life insurance can also be offered to all members of certain insuring groups, regardless of health. Again, groups can range from professional groups to fraternal, religious, or social organizations, to college alumni associations, or even people who are affiliated by financial ties alone.[43]

Yet another strategy if you have difficulty locating adequate life insurance is to accept as much employment-based life insurance as you can get. Convert this insurance to whole life with a reputable company if offered when you leave employment. Some employers offer "conversion" plans for employment-based group term life insurance upon cessation of employment. These conversion plans often require conversion to individual whole life plans. Thus a clever way to get a lot of whole life coverage after diagnosis is to take out a lot of employment group term insurance, then leave your employment after the requisite time and convert it to individual whole life (if your employer makes such an option available). The kicker in these plans is that you usually have to sign up for as much insurance as you can when you begin your job (if you try to add to it later, you will probably be subjected to a physical examination or medical underwriting). This is especially true of federal employment. You can get up to a multiple of five times your salary despite physical health when you begin employment. But if you chose not to take it, you will be subjected to medical underwriting later if you try to get it.

Health Insurance

So where, you wonder, can you find insurance for your chronic illness or disability now that you have already been diagnosed? You should consider the following options:

- If your condition is benign, you may still be insurable by private placement.[44]
- You may be able to obtain an "open enrollment" policy with an insurance company or Blue Cross/Blue Shield if open enrollment plans are available in your state. Call your state insurance commissioner and local Blue Cross/Blue Shield plan to find out what they can offer.[45]
- Although I disfavor this option, you may get your preexisting condition covered through an employer group plan if you can return to work full-time.

[43] In addition to the Internet the best way to find out about these kinds of things is to ask. Discover every group you are or could become a member of. Get yourself on as many mailing lists as possible. Peruse the trade magazines in airports, in doctors' offices, and at county fairs. Junk mail can also be a gold mine.

[44] Two insurance brokerages have indicated that they can place private insurance for people with benign multiple sclerosis. These brokerages are Business Planning Systems Agency, Inc., 3195 Linwood Road, Suite 201, Cincinnatiu, OH 45208; telephone (513) 533-1500 or (800) 423-8496; and Murray and Zuckerman, Inc., P.O. Box 1429, 670 Franklin Street, Schenectady, NY 12301; telephone (518) 382-5483 or (800) 444-0121. Updated listings can be obtained from the book *Who Writes What* published annually by National Underwriter.

[45] Open enrollment is usually time-limited, meaning that there is a time period each year when individuals can enroll in a health insurance program. Several states mandate open enrollment. When a state has mandated open enrollment, there is no high-risk pool. In some states open enrollment is limited to either HMOs or traditional indemnity plans. In other states the state has mandated that both types of plans offer eligibility. Blue Cross/Blue Shield may have additional open enrollment periods not required of other insurance companies. Open enrollment plans may not be as comprehensive as other insurance plans and may be quite expensive. See further discussion of open enrollment below.

If you can only return to work part-time, you may still obtain employer-based health coverage from some employers (notably some temporary agencies).

You may also be able to obtain a large association-based "catastrophic" or "excess" major medical plan (I prefer this as an adjunct to other insurance). [See description of this insurance below.]

- Through government plans such as Medicare or Medicaid (highly disfavored by me).
- Through COBRA continuation coverage after leaving an employer group (generally highly disfavored because of limited continuity or content protection).
- Through state risk pools (also known as CHIPs, TCHIPs, or HIRSP [health insurance risk sharing plan]).[46]
- Through large association "guaranteed issue" health plans. Use the same methodology as discussed above for group life and disability to locate group health coverage through an association plan.
- Through conversion of employer-sponsored plan policy to an individual plan (generally disfavored because of expense and inadequate coverage).
- In states with guaranteed-issue requirements, by forming a small company and hiring help, including yourself, and taking out a small employer's group health plan.[47]
- In states without guaranteed-issue, by forming a small company and hiring help, including yourself, and joining a health-plan purchasing cooperative with adequate coverage.[48]

When evaluating a traditional fee-for-service insurance plan, take specific note of the following:

- Are hospital charges completely covered?
- How much is the deductible?
- How much of the doctors' fees are covered?
- What is and is not covered?
- What is the limit on my out-of-pocket costs?
- What is the maximum lifetime coverage?

---

[46] A number of states have established comprehensive health insurance risk plans. High risk plans guarantee availability of health insurance regardless of the health status of an individual. However, there are generally preexisting conditions and lifetime maximums that apply to these programs. If you are eligible for other insurance coverage, you may not be eligible for the high risk pool. High risk pools are regulated and legislated by individual states, so there may be differences between these programs. Because high risk pools insure only high risk individuals, the cost to these programs are significantly higher than ordinary insurance plans experience. In order properly to fund these programs, many states assess the participating members (insurance companies) an amount proportionate to their share of the health insurance market. Other states subsidize these programs through some form of tax credit against premium taxes or other taxes.

[47] Wisconsin, for example, provides such a guarantee for a company with a worker for at least 30 hours per week, with a two-person company minimum; this law also mandates preexisting coverage for family members.

[48] Institute for Health Policy Solutions (202) 857-0810. This organization will show you how to start your own health plan purchasing cooperative and give you information on existing cooperatives.

- When does coverage begin?
- What is the company's policy about preexisting conditions?
- How long are children covered?
- What are the restrictions on hospitalization and surgery?
- How much does the policy cost?
- Do you have the right to renew?
- Is the insurance company financially sound?

When you are reviewing policies:

- *Do* buy a group policy if possible.
- *Do* take advantage of any "free look" provision when you receive a policy.
- *Don't* replace a policy just because you think it is out-of-date.
- *Don't,* on the other hand, keep policies merely because you've had them a long time.
- *Don't* try to profit by carrying overlapping health insurance policies.
- *Do* purchase major medical along with your basic hospital/medical policy.
- *Don't* purchase dread-disease policies, such as cancer insurance.
- *Don't* hide an illness or condition that could lead to your application being denied.
- *Don't* pay cash.

When evaluating an HMO or PPO plan, be sure to consider the following:

- Is the primary physician board certified or board eligible? What about specialists? What is required in order to see a specialist? Is is possible for a specialist to serve as a primary physician?
- Is the HMO or PPO affiliated with a good hospital?
- Is the organization accredited by a recognized professional organization or considered "qualified" by the US government?
- How strong are the organization and management?
- Is the HMO or PPO in good financial health?
- Can you choose your own doctor?
- Is routine care given by the doctor or delegated to nurse practitioners or physician's assistants?
- Are there incentives that would lead doctors to skimp on care?
- How long does it take to get an appointment?
- Does the HMO or PPO offer a full range of such preventative health services as nutrition and stress-reduction programs?
- What are the provisions to obtain types of necessary care that are not provided within the HMO or PPO?
- What services are not covered? (For example, durable medical equipment?)
- Would you be covered immediately for preexisting conditions and pregnancy?

How much does it cost?

- What happens if you need a doctor outside the HMO or PPO geographic area?
- In case of a disagreement, what is the grievance procedure?

■ CATASTROPHIC OR "EXCESS" MAJOR MEDICAL PLANS

One type of insurance product that can help cover a chronic illness or disability and can still be obtained regardless of preexisting condition is large-group "catastrophic" or "excess" major medical. After a high deductible has been met (usually about $25,000 or $50,000), this product will provide good coverage for a given condition. Do not be put off by the high deductible. These deductibles are not ordinarily measured by the amount that the beneficiary of the policy pays out of pocket —instead they can often also be measured by the amounts that *any other insurer* has paid toward a given condition (including, for example, Medicare, the VA, worker's compensation, or private insurance). For example, a $25,000 revolving 36-month deductible may simply require that $25,000 be paid toward a given health condition within a 36-month period by *any accepted payor (including another insurance company!).* If your health costs have reached the policy deductible in catastrophic-covered expenses to *all* of your payers, you might qualify under the catastrophic plan. In that case, your condition could be declared catastrophic, and would be covered (usually at high percentage or 100 percent coverage) by the catastrophic plan for whatever benefit period the plan covers.

These plans also tend to be inexpensive, so it is not difficult to carry them in addition to a regular major medical plan. For example, it is not uncommon to see good major medical coverage with a catastrophic deductible of $25,000, with about $1 million of maximum coverage, for an annual premium of less than $200, depending on the insured's age. The "catch" is that usually only very large groups offer them, and they will often have waiting periods for preexisting conditions (typically a year or two) if they do not have outright preexisting condition exclusions. Under such a plan with a waiting period, a person with a chronic illness or disability would have to take out the policy, wait one or two years, and then wait during the period while he or she is accumulating deductible expenses. During that time other coverage or savings would have to be used for illness-related health care costs.

However, if such a plan can be located and locked in early in the course of the chronic illness or disability, it can often be the "ticket" that gives the person with the illness or disability the freedom to avoid catastrophic health-insurance related financial problems if the disease progresses. When combined with any other form of health insurance (including employer-sponsored group major medical), such a plan can reduce the overall exposure to health risks to a fixed amount, even in the absence of continuation coverage. This is because the "catastrophic" health expenses, even if paid out of your own pocket, will be "capped" by the amount of the deductible in this plan. Thus, your "catastrophe" becomes financially fixed, and could be covered by your own savings if necessary.

These plans can typically be obtained through large associations or groups. You should check to see if such coverage is available through professional or trade associations, your church, and other types of groups that you are eligible to join.

If you have obtained a good health insurance policy with a waiver or exclusion for your chronic illness or disability, you should also have good coverage for hospitalization for conditions unrelated to your chronic illness or disability. Additionally, if you have obtained a catastrophic major medical policy, hospitalization expenses for your chronic illness or disability may even be covered after any required waiting period and after the catastrophic deductible has been met.

■ CATASTROPHIC HEALTH INSURANCE USE EXAMPLES

Example 1: Jack and Jean are married, and Jack is the primary breadwinner. Their health insurance comes through Jack's employment. Jean is a stay-at-home mother. Jack has been diagnosed with multiple sclerosis (not benign) and is worried that he may eventually be forced to change jobs or leave work altogether. How can Jack plan now for a potential insurance problem?

A: Jack needs to take a long-term view of his health insurance status to achieve optimum results. While he is still relatively healthy, Jack needs to undergo vocational counseling and possible retraining in order to acquire a position he is more likely to be able to keep despite disease progression, and he also needs to look carefully at health insurance coverage for the whole family. As a person with non-benign multiple sclerosis, he should not count on finding primary health coverage that will include his MS in the individual insurance market. One major consideration will be how to cover the rest of the health needs of his family without having to include them in the (probably expensive) type of insurance that will cover his MS. Another consideration is how to insure the MS itself.

Jack should probably begin looking for replacement insurance for non-MS coverage in the individual market now. He needs to get good coverage for reasonable rates with a company that has a strong financial strength rating. He can try to locate such coverage for his whole family and take a "waiver" or "exclusion" for his MS. He should compare both the coverage and costs with what he now gets through his employer's plan. The longer he waits to take it out, the more he will need to consider the possibility that some other family member (or himself) will acquire some other health condition that would have to be excluded later from that policy (or might be completely disqualifying) when he finally applies. On the other hand, if he simply drops the employer insurance, he will lose whatever coverage he currently has for his MS. Jack's best long-term plan is to carry multiple policies and to insure his income with those extra expenses in mind.

If Jack foresees working for a period of years, he might want to consider acquiring a catastrophic plan from a financially strong insurer to cover his MS through a group association guarantee issue policy (in a group that is likely to be around for years). This policy would allow Jack to use the payments from his current employer-sponsored plan to meet the deductible for his catastrophic plan. If he meets the catastrophic deductible while still employed, he will then be free to switch his whole family to a private plan because his MS will be covered by the catastrophic policy.[49] If at some point he leaves his job, he will not suffer through years of uninsurability. On the other hand, if he does not meet the deductible during his employment, he has at least fixed the amount of the liability of his MS to the deductible plus out-of-pocket costs required by that catastrophic plan. His health risk will be at least minimized and quantified for him, and a savings nest egg of the out-of-pocket expenses can substitute for a primary health insurance product if one is not available to him. Of course, Jack could also see if his state has a high risk pool or guaranteed issue group plan available to him after he exhausts his COBRA coverage if he has not qualified under the catastrophic plan. He should keep the catastrophic plan regardless, because if he should ever meet the deductible, he might be able to drop the additional primary coverage for the MS.

Example 2: Mary, a woman in her thirties, has severe multiple sclerosis and has left her employment and applied for Social Security Disability Income (SSDI). She is in the middle of COBRA coverage. If she is awarded SSDI, she will qualify for Medicare when her COBRA coverage runs out. If she is not awarded SSDI, she will have no coverage at all. What should she do?

A: Other than the issue of whether Mary should rethink whether she really needs SSDI, or whether if retrained she could perform some valuable work elsewhere, she needs to begin looking for additional health coverage. Mary should not assume either that Medicare will in fact be awarded or that, if awarded, Medicare will be sufficient for her needs. Assuming that she does qualify, she will need a good Medicare supplement. She should check with her state insurance regulator to find out if there is Medigap coverage for non-elderly disabled in her state and if so, what the coverage content and costs are. If one is not available, she should try to line up coverage through a risk pool or guaranteed issue plan. She should do this right away because many states have lengthy waiting times for such coverage. If she does not qualify for Medicare, Mary will need to find a plan that will cover her health needs when her COBRA expires. She should start looking now for a good group association guaranteed-issue catastrophic plan that she could implement like Jack, above, and sign up for it as soon as possible. She will probably have to suffer through at least a one-year waiting period before she is eligible even to begin accruing her deductible. If her financial resources are small enough, she should check into the availability of Medicaid. Because living in poverty is not a good long-term plan for a person with a disability to maintain quality of life, Mary needs also to think about how she could become productive again.

[49] Jack needs to make sure that his catastrophic policy will cover his MS claim indefinitely after qualification, or that he has sufficient resources to carry him if the claim for catastrophic benefits ends before other coverage or Medicare becomes available. If the catastrophic plan has a time-limited benefit period, he needs to take that into account.

Example 3: Ruth is a nonelderly recipient of SSDI and Medicare and has a Medigap plan. She wants desperately to increase her income by going back to work, but she is afraid of losing her health benefits should she have to quit her job due to illness. She has already suffered through one period of uninsurability before she got her Medicare and does not want to repeat the experience. What should she do?

A: Ruth should use a catastrophic plan as her springboard to employment. She should begin now to look for a group association guaranteed-issue catastrophic plan and take one out as soon as possible. When the deductible is met on that plan, she can take out a private insurance plan with a "waiver" or "exclusion" on her MS, and return to work. Or, if she chooses, Ruth can use the employer's plan (but be warned that if she comes down with some other health condition while on that plan, she will probably have to live through yet another period of uninsurability).[50]

■ HOSPITAL INDEMNITY INSURANCE

There is no question that if your chronic illness progresses, your need for available cash will also increase. However, contrary to popular opinion, if you find yourself hospitalized fairly frequently for reasons related to your chronic illness or disability, you may have a golden opportunity to raise some of that needed cash precisely *because* you are sick and hospitalized.

One insurance product that is typically available *even to people with preexisting conditions* is called "hospital indemnity" insurance. This insurance is usually sold to large group associations. It pays fixed amounts or "indemnities" for each day you are hospitalized. These policies have several characteristics that make them attractive under the right conditions. First, they need not be purchased *before* they become useful. If you are not hospitalized very much, you would be wise merely to begin a file folder with all the information you obtain about such policies for which you may be eligible. At the appropriate time (discussed below), you can sign up for the various policies. Second, many of these policies simply have waiting periods for preexisting conditions, not exclusions. Third, most of these policies are guaranteed renewable and are issued to large groups. Thus, if you file multiple claims, your future coverage or premiums should not be affected. Fourth, these policies seldom have limitations or coordination of benefits provisions. Thus, they typically are "stackable." In other words, if it makes financial sense to have one policy, it may make just as much sense to have 100 or 1,000 such policies (assuming you can afford the premiums). And, these policies will usually pay all benefits directly to you, regardless of any other health coverage you may have. Because you pay the premiums, all proceeds are also nontaxable.

---

[50] Like Jack, Ruth needs to be aware of any limitation on claims periods under her catastrophic plan.

Because these policies will usually pay you in the range from $50 per day to $300 per day (some even double or triple the coverage for ICU stays), it is not difficult to establish eligibility for thousands of tax-free dollars (assuming you paid the premiums) every time you are hospitalized. The real trick is determining how many of these policies you should acquire and when.

To do this, you need to determine the "index" of the various policies you could obtain. Each policy is usually offered for a fixed annual premium amount. By reading the policy, you can determine how many days of hospitalization it would take to recover your annual premium. For example, if your annual premium is $150, and a proposed policy pays $50 per day beginning the second day of hospitalization, you would need to be hospitalized for four days to collect your annual premium back in claims benefits. Your "index" for such a policy would be four. For another example, if your policy costs $200 annually and your policy would pay $125 per day beginning on the third day, you would have to be hospitalized for four days to collect your annual premium back in claims benefits. You should rate each policy similarly, and determine the payment index for each policy. Round all fractions up to the next whole number.

Next, you need to compare the index scores for each policy to your hospitalization history. If your average annual hospitalization rate exceeds the index on each policy and the hospitalization pattern is likely to continue, you should consider applying for that policy (assuming that it will eventually cover your chronic illness or disability). You should purchase no more policies than you can afford even when you are not hospitalized. Of course, if your average annual hospitalization rate is quite high and you find yourself receiving large amounts of money, this can be a virtually limitless strategy. Only your imagination in determining what groups you can join to obtain this coverage will limit the amount of cash you can generate when you are ill. Additionally, if the biggest obstacle to your ability to work is hospitalization, this insurance can even serve as a crude substitute for disability insurance.

Long-Term Care Financing

Reverse Mortgages and Cash Value Life Insurance Loans

If you find that you do not have enough income or liquid assets to pay for long-term services at home, but have enough to disqualify you for Medicaid coverage for home care and cannot make yourself Medicaid-eligible, you must raise enough cash on your own to pay for it. Two good possibilities exist for raising large lump sums of cash if you have a significant amount of whole life insurance or if you have a home with considerable equity in it. The whole life insurance may have a significant enough cash value to provide you with a large lump sum of cash in the way of a policy loan that you would not have to repay until the time of death of the insured person (and then the loans are merely deducted from policy proceeds). You may, however, be required to make annual interest-only payments on the loans. (Check your policy terms for payment provisions.) You can also convert home equity into cash and continue to live in the home as long as you are physically able to do so. The mechanism for doing this is called a "reverse mortgage" and is basically a loan against the value of a home that does not require repayment until the borrower either sells or otherwise permanently leaves the home.[51]

■ ADDITIONAL CONSIDERATIONS

In no event should you attempt to apply for an insurance policy unless you are certain that the policy will be issued—either because of legal rights to obtain coverage or by a contractual promise of the group or carrier to issue the policy. If you should be denied the policy, this information—plus the information you reported on your application—can be turned over to the "great medical computer in the sky" at the Medical Information Bureau. The function of the Medical Information Bureau is to maintain medical information on individuals for insurance companies, similar to the function of credit bureaus. If you would like to check your current status with the bureau, you may request a disclosure form to get your records. This disclosure form may be obtained by writing to:

Medical Information Bureau
P.O. Box 105
Essex Station
Boston, MA 02112

[51] Information about reverse mortgages in your area can be obtained with $1.00 and a self-addressed stamped envelope from:

National Center for Home Equity Conversion
Reverse Mortgage Locator
7373 147th Street, Suite 115
Apple Valley, MN 55124

RESOURCES

Insurance Rating Agencies

A.M. Best	(800) 424-BEST
Website:	http://www.ambest.com/bestline/index.html
Fitch	(312) 368-3198
Website	http://www.fitchratings.com
Moody's	(212) 553-0377
Website:	http://www.moodys.com
Standard & Poor's	(212) 208-1527
Website:	http://data.insure.com/ratings/sandp.cfm
Weiss Ratings	(800) 289-9222
Website:	http://www.weissratings.com
HMO Rating (NCQA)	http://www.ncqaorg (see section on health plan report card) (see below under organizations)

Organizations

American Association of Retired Persons ("AARP") disseminates valuable information on all types of insurance (202-434-2277). To order their publication *Before You Buy: A Guide to Long-Term Care Insurance* (#D12893), contact AARP at 601 E Street, NW, Washington, DC 20049. (http://www.aarp.org)

Center for Medicare Advocacy is a private nonprofit agency that provides assistance to people with disabilities (and their advocates) in areas of Medicare, educational materials, home care, and referrals. (860-456-7790) (http://www.medicareadvocacy.org)

Center for the Study of Services ("CSS") ranks managed care plans and publishes its findings. 733 15th Street, N.W., Suite 820, Washington, DC 20005; (800-475-7283). CSS publishes an online consumer's checkbook, including information on health plans, services, and insurance. (http://www.checkbook.org/newhig2/hig.cfm).

Consumer Federation of America ("CFA") (202-387-6121 or 0087) is a formidable insurance consumer advocacy group. It publishes a useful life insurance guide, *Taking a Bite Out of Insurance,* which can be obtained for $13.95 (1424 16th Street, NW, Suite 604, Washington, DC 20036). (http//www.consumerfed.org/index.html)

Health Insurance Association of America ("HIAA") has useful booklets for consumers, such as *A Consumer's Guide to Medicare Supplemental Insurance* (202-824-1600). (http://www.hiaa.org)

National Academy of Elder Law Attorneys ("NAELA") (1604 N. Country Club Road, Tucson, AZ 85716; tel: 602-881-4005). If you send them a stamped, self-addressed, legal-sized envelope, they will send you a brochure entitled *Questions and Answers When Looking for an Elder Law Attorney.* (http://www.naela.com)

National Association of Personal Financial Advisors (800-366-2732). They will send you names of association members in your area. (http://www.napfa.org)

National Center for Home Equity Conversion (Reverse Mortgage Locator, National Center for Home Equity Conversion, 7373 147th Street, Suite 115, Apple Valley, MN 66124; tel. 612-953-4474).

National Committee for Quality Assurance ("NCQA") (800-839-6487). NCQA collects information on managed care plans, including HMOs and rates them on factors such as physician credentials and subscriber turnover; it then publishes its findings and accredits the plans. It provides an accreditation status report for free. This report can also be accessed via NCQA's web site (http://www.ncqa.org).

US News and World Report ranked 230 HMO Plans in 46 states, and provides the information on their website at http//www.usnews.com; search the website for "HMO Rankings"

National Information Center for Children and Youth with Disabilities ("NICHCY") (P.O. Box 1492, Washington, D.C. 20013-1492; tel: 800-695-0285; 202-884-8200). (http://www.kidsource.com/NICHCY/INDEX.HTML)

People's Medical Society publishes useful information about health insurance (610-770-1670). (http://www.peoplesmed.org)

United Seniors Health Council, Department PG3, 1331 H Street, NW, Washington, DC 20005-4706 publishes *Long Term Care Insurance: A Professional's Guide to Selecting Policies,* by Susan Polniaszek and James Firman. This 110-page book is available for $41.00. (http://www.unitedseniorshealth.org) It also publishes a number of other helpful books and pamphlets on insurance planning.

The Joint Committee on Accreditation ("JCAHO") reports on preferred provider organizations. (http://www.jcaho.org)

American Association of Health Plans ("AAHP") has established standards for health plans. 1129 20th street NW, Suite 600, Washington D.C. 20036-341; (202) 778-3200 (http://www.aahp.org)

Magazines

Resource directory for parents of children with disabilities in the September 1996 issue of ***Exceptional Parent.***

Health Pages Magazine is a consumer's guide to managed care, 135 Fifth Avenue, New York, NY 10010. (212) 505-0103

Books

Bamford, J., *Smarter Insurance Solutions.* Princeton: Bloomberg Press, 1996.
Before You Buy: A Guide to Long-Term Care Insurance (publication #D12893) Available from: AARP, 601 E. St. NW, Washington, DC 20049.
Brown, C. *100 Questions Every Working American Must Ask.* Chicago: Dearborn Financial Publishing, 1996.
Davidson, C. *The Over 50 Insurance Survival Guide.* Santa Monica: Merritt Publishing, 1994.
Garner RJ, Coplan RB, Raasch BJ, Ratner, CL, *Ernst & Young's Personal Financial Planning Guide.* New York: John Wiley & Sons, 1995.
Isaacs SL, Swartz AC, *The Consumer's Guide to Today's Health Care.* New York: Houghton Mifflin, 1992.
Long-Term Care Insurance: A Professional's Guide to Selecting Policies, by Susan Polniaszek and James Firman (1981), available from United Seniors Health Cooperative, Department PG3, 1331 H Street, NW, Suite 500, Washington, DC 20005-4706.
Matthews J. *Beat the Nursing Home Trap: A Consumer's Guide to Choosing & Financing Long-Term Care* (2nd edition). Berkeley, Calif.: Nolo Press, 1993.
Mendelsohn S. *Tax Options and Strategies for People with Disabilities* (2nd edition). New York: Demos, 1996.
Pond JD. *The New Century Family Money Book.* New York: Dell Publishing, 1993.
Quinn, JB. *Making the Most of Your Money.* New York: Simon & Schuster, 1997.
Roberts R. *The Veterans Guide to Benefits.* New York: Signet, 1989.
Russell LM, Grant AE, Joseph SM, Fee RW. *Planning for the Future: Providing a Meaningful Life for a Child with a Disability After Your Death* (2nd edition). Evanston, Ill.: American Publishing, 1993.

Web Sites

Laura's Links: An extensive continually-updating Website developed by the author providing links to other sites to aid in insurance and risk planning, and to obtain general information that may be helpful in the planning process: **http//www.lauraslinks.com**

Insurance News Network ("INN") (http://www.insure.com) is an independent, online news service with an abundance of valuable consumer information. For example, INN carries data from state insurance departments, has links to insurance financial health rating agencies, and has some premium surveys.

InsWeb allows you to comparison shop for insurance and compare quotes in cyberspace (http://www.insweb.com)

APPENDIX 1

States & Territories Contact Information

updates my be available on
http://www.hsh.com/pamphlets/state_ins_depts.html

Insurance Regulator Information			
State or Territory	***Address***	***Telephone***	***World Wide Web***
Alabama	Insurance Commissioner 201 Monroe Street, Suite 1700 Montgomery, AL 36130-3351	(334) 269-3550	http://www.aldoi.org
Alaska	Division of Insurance Director of Insurance P.O. Box 110805 Juneau, AK 99811-0805	(907)465-2515	http:/lwww.dced.state.ak.us./insurance
Arizona	Arizona Dept. of Insurance 2910 North 44th St., Suite 210 Phoenix, AZ 85018-7156	(602) 912-8444	http://www.state.az.us/id
Arkansas	Arkansas Insurance Dept. 1200 West 3rd St. Little (800) 282-9134 Rock, AR 72201-1904	(501) 371-2600	http://www.state.ar.us/insurance/
California	California Dept. of Insurance Consumer Communications Bureau 300 South Spring St., South Tower Angeles, CA 90013	(415) 538-4040 (San Francisco) (213) 346-6400 (Los Angeles)	http://www.insurance.ca.gov/docs
Colorado	Colorado Division of Insurance 1560 Broadway, Suite 850 Denver, CO 80202	(303) 894-7499	http://www.dora.state.co.us/Insurance
Connecticut	Insurance Department P.O. Box 816 Hartford, CT 06142-0816	(860) 297-3802	http://www.state.ct.us/cid
Delaware	Delaware Dept. of Insurance 841 Silver Lake Blvd. P.O. Box 7007 Dover, DE 19903	(302) 739-4251	http://www.state.de.us/inscom
District of Columbia	Insurance Administration District of Columbia Government 441 Fourth St. NW 8th Floor North Washington, DC 20001	(202) 727-8000 x301 8	http://dist.washingtondc.gov/main.shtm
Florida	Florida Dept. of Insurance State Capitol Plaza Level Eleven Tallahassee, FL 32399-0300	(850) 922-3101	http://www.doi.state.fl.us/
Georgia	Georgia Dept. of Insurance 2 Martin L. king, Jr. Drive Floyd Memorial Building West Tower, Suite 704 Atlanta, GA 30334	(404) 656-2056	http://www.InsComm.State.Ga.US/

State or Territory	Address	Telephone	World Wide Web
Guam	Dept. of Revenue & Taxation Government of Guam Building 13-1, 2nd Floor Mariner Avenue Tiyan, Barrigada, GU 96913	(671) 475-1817	http://mail.admin.gov.gu/revtax/ins.html
Hawaii	Hawaii Insurance Division Dept. of Commerce & Consumer Affair 250 S. king St., 5th Floor Honolulu, HI 96813	(808) 586-2790	http://www.state.hi.us/dcca/ins/
Idaho	Director of Insurance West State St., 3rd Floor P.O. Box 93720 Boise, ID 83720-0043	700 (208) 334-4250	http://www.doi.state.id.us/
Illinois	Illinois Department of Insurance 320 W. Washington St. 4th Floor Springfield, IL 62767-0001	(217) 782-4515	http://www.state.il.us/ins/default.htm
Indiana	Indiana Dept. of Insurance 311 W. Washington St., Ste 300 Indianapolis, IN 46204-2787	(317) 232-2385	http://www.state.in.us/idoi/
Iowa	Iowa Division of Insurance Lucas State Ofce Bldg., 6th Floor Des Moines, IA 50319-0065	(515)281-5705	http://www.iid.state.ia.us/
Kansas	kansas Department of Insurance State of Kansas 420 S.W. 9th Street Topeka, KS 66612-1678	(785) 296-7801	http://www.ksinsurance.org/
Kentucky	Kentucky Dept. of Insurance 215 W. Main St. P.O. Box 517 Frankfort, KY 40602-0517	(502) 564-6027	http://www.doi state.ky.us/
Louisiana	Louisiana Dept. of Insurance 950 N. 5th St. Baton Rouge, LA 70802	(225) 342-5423	http://wwwldi.ldi.state.la.us/
Maine	Department of Professional & Financial Regulation Maine Bureau of Insurance State Office Building Station 34 Augusta, ME 04333-0034	(207) 624-8475	http://www.state.me.us/pfr/ins/inshome2.ht
Maryland	Maryland Insurance Admin. 501 St. Paul P1., 7th Flr. So. Baltimore, MD 21202-2272	(410) 468-2090	http://www.mdinsurance.state.md.us/
Massachusetts	Division of Insurance Commonwealth of Massachusetts 470 Atlantic Avenue Boston, MA 02210-2223	(617) 521-7794	http://www.magnet.state.ma.us/ofis
Michigan	Michigan Insurance Bureau Department. of Commerce 611 W. Ottawa St., 2nd Flr North Lansing, MI 48933-1020	(517) 373-9273	http://www.cis.state.mi.us/ofis/
Minnesota	Minnesota Dept. of Commerce Insurance Division 133 E. 7th St. St. Paul, MN 55101	(612) 296-6848	http://www.commerce.state.mn.us/

State or Territory	Address	Telephone	World Wide Web
Mississippi	Mississippi Dept. of Insurance 550 High Street P.O. Box 79 Jackson, MS 39201	(601) 359-3569	http://www.doi.state.ms.us/
Missouri	Missouri Dept. of Insurance 301 West High St., 6 North Jefferson City, MO 65102-0690	(573) 751-4126	http://insurance.state.mo.us/
Montana	Montana Dept. of Insurance 126 North Sanders Mitchell Building, Room 270 Helena, MT 59601	(406) 444-2040	http://www.mt.gov/sao/insdiv.htm
Nebraska	Nebraska Dept. of Insurance Terminal Building 941 "O" St., Suite 400 Lincoln, NE 68508-3690	(402) 471-2201	http://www.nol .org/home/NDOI/
Nevada	Nevada Division of Insurance 1665 Hot Springs Rd., Suite 152 Carson City, NV 89710	(702) 687-4270	http://www.doi.state.nv.us/
New Hampshire	NH Dept. of Insurance Manchester St. Concord, NH 03301	169 (603) 271-2261	http://www.state.nh.us/insurance/
New Jersey	New Jersey Dept. of Insurance 20 West State St. CN325 Trenton, NJ 08625	(609) 292-5363	http://states.naic.org/ni/NJHOMEPG.HTML http://www.state.nj.us/dobi/index.html
New Mexico	New Mexico Dept. of Insurance P.O. Drawer 1269 Santa Fe, NM 87504-1269	(505) 827-4500	htp://www.nmprc.state.nm.us/inshm.htm
New York	New York Dept. of Insurance State of New York Consumer Bureau 25 Beaver Street New York, NY 10004-2319	(212) 480-2287	http://www.ins.state.ny.us/
North Carolina	North Carolina Dept. of Insurance P.O. Box 26387 Raleigh, NC 27611	(919) 733-7349	http://www.ncdoi.com/
North Dakota	North Dakota Dept. of Insurance 600 East Boulevard Ave. Bismarck, ND 58505-0320	(919) 733-7349	http://www.state.nd.us/ndins/
Ohio	Ohio Dept. of Insurance 2100 Stella Court Columbus, OH 43215-1067	(614) 644-2658	http://www.ohioinsurance.gov/
Oklahoma	Oklahoma Dept. of Insurance 3814 North Santa Fe Oklahoma City, OK 73118	(405) 521-2828	http://www.oid.state.ok.us/
Oregon	Oregon Division of Insurance Dept. Consumer & Bus. Services 350 Winter St. NE, Room 200 Salem, OR 97310-0700	(503) 947-7980	http://www.cbs.state.or.us/external/ins/index.html
Pennsylvania	Pennsylvania Insurance Dept. 1326 Strawberry Square 13th Floor Harrisburg, PA 17120	(717) 783-0442	http://www.insurance.state.pa.us/
Puerto Rico	Puerto Rico Dept. of Insurance Cobian's Plaza Bldg. 1607 Ponce de Leon Avenue Santurce, PR 00909	(787) 722-8686	

State or Territory	Address	Telephone	World Wide Web
Rhode Island	Rhode Island Insurance Div. Dept. of Business Regulation 233 Richmond St., Suite 233 Providence, RI 02903-4233	(401)277-2223	http://www.dbr.state.ri.us/
South Carolina	SC Dept. of Insurance 1612 Marion St. P.O. Box 100105 Columbia, SC 29201	(803) 737-6160	http://www.state.sc.us:80/doi/
South Dakota	SD Division of Insurance Dept. of Commerce & Regulation 118 W. Capitol Ave. Pierre, SD 57501-2000	(605) 773-3563	http://www.state.sd.us/dcr/insurance/
Tennessee	TN Dept. of Commerce & Ins. 500 James Robertston Prkwy Volunteer Plaza Nashville, TN 37243-0565	(615)741-2241	http://www.state.tn.us/commerce/
Texas	Texas Dept of Insurance 333 Guadalupe Street P.O. Box 149104 Austin, TX 78714-9104	(512) 463-6464	http //www.tdi.state.tx.us/
Utah	Utah Department of Insurance State Office Bldg. Rm. 3110 Salt Lake City, UT 84114-1201	(801) 538-3800	http://www.insurance.state.ut.us/
Vermont	Vermont Division of Insurance Dept Banking, Insurance & Sec. 89 Main St., Drawer 20 Montpelier, VT 05620-3101	(802) 828-3301	http://www.bishca.state.vt.us/
Virgin Islands	Division of Banking & Insurance 1131 King Street Christiansted St. Croix, VI 00820	(809) 773-6449	e-mail: vidoi001@aol.com
Virginia	Virginia Bureau of Insurance State Corporation Coommission 1300 East Main Street Richmond, VA 23219	(804) 371-9694	http://www.state.va.us/scc/division/boi/index.htm
Washington	Washington Office of the Insurance Commissioner, 14th & Water Strteets P0 Box 40255 Olympia, WA 98504-0255	(360) 753-7301	http://www.insurance.wa.gov/
West Virginia	West VA Dept. of Insurance P0 Box 50540 Charleston, WV 25305-0540	(304) 558-3354	http://www.state.wv.us/insurance/
Wisconsin	Office of the Commissioner of Insurance State of Wisconsin 121 East Wilson Madison, WI 53702	(608) 266-0102	http://badger.state.wi.us/agencies/oci/oci/home.htm
Wyoming	Wyoming Dept. of Insurance Herschler Building 122 W. 25th St., 3rd East Cheyenne, WY 82002-0440	(307) 777-7401	http://insurance.state.wy.us/

APPENDIX 2

Summary Comparison of Individual Market Reforms in 50 States and the District of Columbia

INDIVIDUAL MARKET REFORMS

	Guaranteed issue	Guaranteed renewability	Preexisting condition exclusion limits (months)	Definition of preexisting condition	Lookback period limits (months)	Credit for prior coverage	Maximum gap in prior coverage (days)	Rating restrictions	Standardized benefit package required?	Special rules for federal eligibles	Other reforms
AL	none	yes	no limit at time of issue, 2 years for conditions arising after coverage begins	objective standard	no limit at time of issue, 5 years for conditions arising after coverage begins	no	n/a	no restrictions*	no	high risk pool for federal eligibles only, two coverage options with no pre-ex	
AK	none	yes	no limit	prudent person (any condition for which the plan judges most people would have sought care)	no limit	no	n/a	no restrictions*	no	access to high risk pool with no pre-ex	high risk pool for "uninsurables"
AZ	none	yes	no limit	objective standard (only those conditions for which the individual actually sought care)	no limit	no	n/a	no restrictions*	no	HIPAA standard (guaranteed issue of at least 2 plans with benefits similar to plans sold to other consumers, no pre-ex); all products if insurers do not designate 2 plans, no rating limits*	mandatory group conversion without rating limits*
AR	none	yes	12, generally 6, specific medical conditions	prudent person (see AK for def.)	5 years	no	n/a	no restrictions*	no	access to high risk pool with no pre-ex	high risk pool for "uninsurables;" mandatory group conversion without rating limits*
CA	none	yes	1-2 people covered--12 months; 3 or more--6 months	objective standard (see AZ for def.)	12 if 1-2 people covered; 6 if 3 or more covered	yes	63 or 180, depending on situation	no restrictions*	no	HIPAA standard (see AZ); 2 plans must be federally-approved, no rating limits*	high risk pool for "uninsurables;" mandatory group conversion without rating limits*

CO	none	yes	12, elimination riders allowed	objective standard (see AZ for def.)	12	yes	90	no restrictions*	no	HIPAA standard (see AZ); all products if insurers do not designate 2 plans, no rating limits*	high risk pool for "uninsurables"
CT	none	yes	12	objective standard (see AZ for def.)	12	yes	63	no restrictions*	no	access to high risk pool with no pre-ex	high risk pool for "uninsurables;" mandatory group conversion without rating limits*
DC	some (annual 6 month BC/BS open enrollment)	yes	no limit (plans with pre-ex periods must be reviewed by Dept. of Insurance), elimination riders permitted	prudent person (see AK for def.)	no limit	no	n/a	no restrictions*	no	HIPAA standard (see AZ), all products if insurers do not designate 2 plans, no rating limits*	
DE	none	yes	no limit	not defined	no limit	no	n/a	no restrictions*	no	HIPAA standard (see AZ), all products if insurers do not designate 2 plans, no rating restrictions*	

	Guaranteed issue	Guaranteed renewability	Preexisting condition exclusion limits (months)	Definition of preexisting condition	Lookback period limits (months)	Credit for prior coverage	Maximum gap in prior coverage (days)	Rating restrictions	Standardized benefit package required?	Special rules for federal eligibles	Other reforms
FL	none	yes	insurers may impose 2 year pre-ex (with credit for prior coverage) or may use permanent exclusions	prudent person (see AK for def.)	2 years	only if qualify for plan with 2 year pre-ex	62	no restrictions*	no	federal eligibles with prior fully insured group coverage qualify for conversion policies; federal eligibles with prior self-insured coverage are entitled to 2 most popular products or conversion policies, at insurer's option; no pre-ex for any federal eligible; rating limits for those federal eligibles who purchase conversion policies.	mandatory group conversion with rating limits
GA	none	yes	2 years with elimination riders permitted	not defined	no limit	no	n/a	no restrictions*	no	federal eligibles with prior fully insured group coverage can buy enhanced conversion policy (choice of 2 plans), no pre-ex, rating limits; federal eligibles with prior self-insured coverage have access to 2 standard plans from insurer assigned by state, no pre-ex, rating limits	mandatory group conversion with rating limits

HI	some; Kaiser and other large insurers guarantee issue	yes	no limit (but Kaiser and other large insurers don't pre-ex)	not defined	no limit	no	n/a	no restrictions* (but Kaiser and other large insurers community rate)	no	HIPAA standard (see AZ), all products if insurers do not designate 2 plans, no rating restrictions* (but Kaiser and other large insurers community rate)	subsidized coverage for low income individuals through Hawaii Quest
ID**	some (basic, standard, and catastrophic policies for those with prior coverage, open enrollment for those without prior coverage)	yes	12	prudent person (see AK for def.)	6	yes	63	rate bands	yes, basic, standard, and catastrophic; other plans permitted	same access as other residents	mandatory group conversion with rating limits
IL	none	yes	no limit	prudent person (see AK for def.)	no limit	no	n/a	no restrictions*	no	access to high risk pool with no pre-ex; pool offers 2 plans exclusively for federal eligibles with premiums and benefits similar to other plans	high risk pool for "uninsurables;" mandatory group conversion without rating limits*
IN	none	yes	12	prudent person (see AK for def.)	12	yes, credit for prior small group coverage only	30	no restrictions*	no	access to high risk pool with no pre-ex	high risk pool for "uninsurables;" mandatory group conversion with rating limits

	Guaranteed issue	Guaranteed renewability	Preexisting condition exclusion limits (months)	Definition of preexisting condition	Lookback period limits (months)	Credit for prior coverage	Maximum gap in prior coverage (days)	Rating restrictions	Standardized benefit package required?	Special rules for federal eligibles	Other reforms
IA	some (basic and standard plans if 12 months prior coverage, either through high risk pool or from private insurers depending on type of prior coverage)	yes	12	prudent person (see AK for def.)	6	yes	63	rate bands	yes, basic and standard; other plans permitted	if not eligible for standard or basic, access to high risk pool with no pre-ex	high risk pool for "uninsurables;" after 12 months, re-enter private market; mandatory group conversion without rating limits*
KS	none	yes	24, elimination riders allowed	prudent person (see AK for def.)	no limit	no	n/a	no restrictions*	no	access to high risk pool with no pre-ex	high risk pool for "uninsurables;" mandatory group conversion without rating limits*
KY**	some (all products for 12 month residents without serious health conditions, 1-2 plans in Guaranteed Acceptance Program for those with serious health conditions)	yes	12	objective standard (see AZ for def.)	6	yes	63	rate bands	yes, standard plan; other plans permitted	access to any individual plan from any insurer with no pre-ex	Guaranteed Acceptance Program for individuals with serious health conditions; mandatory group conversion without rating limits*
LA	none	yes	12	prudent person (see AK for def.)	12	yes	63	rate bands	no	access to high risk pool with no pre-ex, no wait list, premiums higher for federal eligibles	high risk pool for "uninsurables"

ME	all products (60-day residency requirement)	yes	12	prudent person (see AK for def.)	12	yes	90	modified community rating	yes, basic and standard; other plans permitted	same access as other residents, except no residency requirement or pre-ex	
MD	some (semi annual SAAC open enrollment period)	yes	24, none for HMOs	prudent person (see AK for def.), n/a to HMOs	7 years, n/a to HMOs	no	n/a	no restrictions except SAAC premiums may not vary by health status	no	HIPAA standard (see AZ); all products if insurers do not designate 2 plans; rate limits only for high and low option plans	mandatory group conversion without rating limits*
MA	some (all products, some individuals only during open enrollment)	yes	0	carrier's option of prudent person or objective standard	0	n/a	n/a	modified community rating	minimum standardized benefits	same access as for other individuals	optional conversion, no rating limits
MI	some (BC/BS guarantee issue to all residents)	yes	12, 6 for HMO or BC/BS	objective standard (see AZ for def.)	6	no, but some insurers waive pre-ex if individual is leaving certain types of group coverage	n/a	community rating for BC/BS plans; no restrictions for other plans*	no	access to 2 BC/BS plans with no pre-ex or probationary periods, all products if insurers do not designate 2 plans	mandatory group conversion without rating limits*
MN	some (HMO annual open enrollment for HMOs operating >2 years in MN)	yes	12	objective standard (see AZ for def.)	6	yes	63	rate bands, no increases due to health status upon renewal	no	access to high risk pool with no pre-ex	high risk pool for "uninsurables;" Minnesota-Care program for low income residents; mandatory group conversion with rating limits*

	Guaranteed issue	Guaranteed renewability	Preexisting condition exclusion limits (months)	Definition of preexisting condition	Lookback period limits (months)	Credit for prior coverage	Maximum gap in prior coverage (days)	Rating restrictions	Standardized benefit package required?	Special rules for federal eligibles	Other reforms
MS	none	yes	12, elimination riders permitted	prudent person (see AK for def.)	12	no	n/a	no restrictions*	no	access to high risk pool with no pre-ex	high risk pool for "uninsurables"
MO	none	yes	2 years	not defined	no limit	no	n/a	no restrictions*	no	HIPAA standard (see AZ), all products if insurers do not designate 2 plans	high risk pool for "uninsurables;" mandatory group conversion without rating limits*
MT	none	yes	12; elimination riders permitted	objective standard (see AZ for def.)	3 years	yes	30	no restrictions*	yes	access to high risk pool with no pre-ex, 2 plans exclusively for federal eligibles with benefits slightly more expansive than regular pool coverage	high risk pool for "uninsurables;" mandatory group conversion with rating limits for some plans
NE	none	yes	no limit	prudent person (see AK for def.)	no limit	no	n/a	no restrictions*	no	access to high risk pool with no pre-ex	high risk pool for "uninsurables"
NV	none	yes	no limit	prudent person (see AK for def.)	no limit	no	n/a	rate bands	yes, for federal eligibles (basic and standard)	federal eligibles can buy standard and basic plans; same rating limits that apply to regular individual market products apply	mandatory group conversion with rating limits (optional for HMOs)
NH	all products	yes	9; 3 if no medical expenses for pre-ex condition in first 3 months of coverage	objective standard (see AZ for def.)	3	yes	63	rate bands	no	same access as other residents	
NJ	all products	yes	12	prudent person (see AK for def.)	6	yes	31	community rating	yes, exclusively	same access as other residents, except 63-day maximum gap in coverage	all licensed insurers must sell individual coverage or subsidize losses of carriers that do; 75% minimum los ratio; strong public education effort

NM	none	yes	6	prudent person (see AK for def.)	6	yes	31	rate bands, modified community rating in Alliance	no	federal eligibles can buy guaranteed issue coverage through high risk pool or small employer Health Insurance Alliance, no pre-ex	high risk pool for "uninsurables;" mandatory group conversion without rating limits*
NY	all products	yes	12, generally 10, pregnancy	objective standard (see AZ for def.)	6	yes	63	community rating	yes, HMOs must offer 2 standardized plans (HMO and point-of-service), other plans permitted	same access as other residents. Plans cannot include any pre ex condition standards	mandatory group conversion with rating limits
NC	none	yes	12	objective standard (see AZ for def.)	12	yes	63	no restrictions*	no	HIPAA standard (see AZ), all products if insurers do not designate 2 plans	mandatory group conversion without rating limits*
ND	none	yes	12	objective standard (see AZ for def.)	6	yes	63	modified community rating	yes, basic and standard; other plans permitted	access to high risk pool with no pre-ex	high risk pool for "uninsurables;" mandatory group conversion in some situations, no rating limits*
OH	some (annual open enrollment with state-approved enrollment caps)	yes	12	prudent person (see AK for def.)	6	yes	30	rate bands	yes, basic and standard; other plans permitted	access to basic and standard conversion or private individual products similar to plans sold to small employers, no pre-ex, rating limits specific to federal eligibles	mandatory group conversion with rating limits

	Guaranteed issue	Guaranteed renewability	Preexisting condition exclusion limits (months)	Definition of preexisting condition	Lookback period limits (months)	Credit for prior coverage	Maximum gap in prior coverage (days)	Rating restrictions	Standardized benefit package required?	Special rules for federal eligibles	Other reforms
OK	none	yes	no limit for indemnity, 0 for HMOs	prudent person (see AK for def.)	no limit for indemnity, 0 for HMOs	no	n/a	no restrictions for indemnity plans, modified community rating for HMOs	no	access to high risk pool with no pre-ex	high risk pool for "uninsurables;" 30-day extension of group (indemnity) coverage upon termination
OR	some (portability plans for individuals with 6 months prior coverage)	yes	0 for portability plans; 6 months for other plans (or may use 90-day waiting period)	objective standard (see AZ for def.)	0 for portability plans; 6 for others	yes	63	modified community rating	yes, portability plans; other plans permitted	access to portability plans through high risk pool or private insurers (depending on type of prior coverage)	high risk pool for "uninsurables"
PA	some (BC/BS guarantee issue to all residents)	yes	12, probationary periods allowed in some situations	objective standard (see AZ for def.)	5 years	no, BC/BS may give credit for prior BC/BS coverage	n/a	no restrictions* on initial rates, may not reclassify individuals into higher risk classes due to health upon renewal; BC/BS community rate as matter of practice	no	access to 2 BC/BS plans with no pre-ex or probationary periods, all products if insurers do not designate 2 plans	mandatory group conversion with rating limits

RI	some (all products for residents with 12 months prior coverage with no gap)	yes	3 years for insurers other than HMOs or BC/BS (HMOs and BC/BS usually impose shorter pre-ex), none for guaranteed issue plans when benefit was covered under prior coverage	prudent person (see AK for def.)	36	no (but no pre-ex for g issue plans)	n/a	no restrictions*	no	HIPAA standard (see AZ), all products if insurers do not designate 2 plans	mandatory group conversion without rating limits*
SC	none	yes	12 for HMOs; for others, range is 12 months to permanent, depending on whether plan asks medical questions at time of application	prudent person (see AK for def.)	12 for HMOs; for others, 12 months to 5 years, depending on whether plan asks medical questions at time of application	no	n/a	no restrictions*	no	access to high risk pool with no pre-ex	high risk pool for "uninsurables;" mandatory group conversion for divorced spouses without rating limits
SD	some (2 plans for residents with at least 12 months prior coverage)	yes	12	prudent person (see AK for def.)	12	yes	63	rate bands	yes, basic and standard; other plans permitted	same access as other residents; conversion coverage only counts as creditable coverage for federal eligibles	mandatory group conversion with rating limits
TN	none	yes	2 years, but permanent exclusions allowed for specific conditions	prudent person (see AK for def.)	no limit	no	n/a	no restrictions*	no	HIPAA standard (see AZ), all products if insurers do not designate 2 plans	TennCare program for certain uninsured children and dislocated workers; mandatory group conversion without rating limits*

	Guaranteed issue	Guaranteed renewability	Preexisting condition exclusion limits (months)	Definition of preexisting condition	Lookback period limits (months)	Credit for prior coverage	Maximum gap in prior coverage (days)	Rating restrictions	Standardized benefit package required?	Special rules for federal eligibles	Other reforms
TX	none	yes	24, elimination riders allowed	prudent person (see AK for def.)	5 years	yes, up to 18 months if most recent prior coverage was in employer group plan	not specified	no restrictions*	no	access to high risk pool with no pre-ex, elimination riders still permitted	high risk pool for "uninsurables"
UT	none	yes	12	objective standard (see AZ for def.)	6	yes	62	rate bands	no	access to high risk pool with no pre-ex, private coverage if pool reaches enrollment cap	high risk pool for "uninsurables;" mandatory group conversion without rating limits*
VT	yes, all plans (VT residents)	yes	12, 0 if 9 months creditable coverage	objective standard (see AZ for def.)	6	yes	63	community rating	yes, other plans permitted	same access as other residents	
VA	some (BC/BS guarantee issue to all residents)	yes	12	carrier's option of prudent person or objective standard	12	yes	30	no restrictions*	no	guaranteed issue of all individual products from all insurers with no pre-ex	mandatory group conversion without rating limits*
WA**	none	yes	9	objective standard (see AZ for def.) and prudent layperson (see AK for def.)	6	yes	63	modified community rating	no	same access as other residents	low-income subsidies available for Basic Health Plan; high risk pool for 'uninsurables" and for residents in counties where no individual comprehensive coverage is sold
WV	some (semi-annual HMO open enrollment periods)	yes	12, elimination riders allowed	prudent person (see AK for def.)	2 years	yes	63	no restrictions*	no	HIPAA standard (see AZ), all products if insurers do not designate 2 plans	mandatory group conversion without rating limits*

WI	none	yes	no limit, can impose elimination riders	"relating to a condition of an individual that existed before the individual's date of enrollment"	no limit	no	n/a	no restrictions*	no	access to high risk pool with no pre-ex	high risk pool for "uninsurables;" mandatory group conversion without rating limits*
WY	none	yes	12	objective standard (see AZ for def.)	6	yes	90	no restrictions*	no	access to high risk pool with no pre-ex	high risk pool for "uninsurables;" mandatory group conversion without rating limits*

* rates may still be subject to some state oversight, such as requirement that rates be actuarially justifiable.
** recent statutory changes may not be reflected by this chart.

SMALL GROUP MARKET REFORMS

	Definition of small group	Guaranteed issue all products	Guaranteed renewability	Preexisting condition exclusion limits (months)	Lookback period limits (months)	Maximum gap in prior coverage (days)	Rating restrictions	Standardized plans required?	Mini-COBRA coverage (months)	Other reforms
AL	2-50	Yes	Yes	12	6	63	adjusted community	no	none	
AK	2-50	Yes	Yes	12	6	63 self-insured, 90 fully insured	rate bands	yes	none	mandatory small employer reinsurance program
AZ	2-50, 1 for g-issue of 1 plan	Yes	Yes	12	6	63	modified community rating for Health Care Group (HCG), rate bands for all others	no	none	state-run program (HCG) for small employers that meet eligibility requirements, elective small employer reinsurance program
AR	2-50, 1 eligible for small group, but no g-issue	Yes	Yes	12, regular enrollee 18, late enrollee	6	63	rate bands for groups of 2-25	no	120 days	
CA	2-50	Yes	Yes	12 self-insured, 6 fully insured	6	63 self-insured, 180 some fully insured	rate bands	no	18	elective small employer reinsurance program
CO	2-50, 1 for g-issue of 2 plans	Yes	Yes	12 self-insured, 6 fully insured	6	63 self-insured, 90 fully insured	modified community rating	yes, other plans permitted	18	elective small employer reinsurance program

CT	1-50	Yes	Yes	12	6	63 self-insured, 90 fully insured	modified community rating	yes, other plans permitted	24 months, but 3 years if spouse has died or marriage dissolved	mandatory small employer reinsurance program
DC	2-50	Yes	Yes	12	6	63	no restrictions*	no	none	
DE	1-50	Yes	Yes	12	6	63	rate bands	yes, other plans permitted	none	elective small employer reinsurance program
FL	1-50	Yes	Yes	12	6	63	modified community rating	yes, other plans permitted	18	small employer purchasing alliance, elective small employer program
GA	2-50	Yes	Yes	12	6	63 self-insured, 90 fully insured	rate bands	no	3	
HI	2-50	Yes	Yes	0	0	0	no restrictions,* except community rating for HMSA & Kaiser	no	none	employee mandate
ID	2-50	Yes	Yes	12	6	63	rate bands	yes, other plans permitted	none	elective small employer reinsurance program
IL	2-50	Yes	Yes	12	6	63	rate bands (eff. 7/1/2000)	no	9	
IN	2-50	Yes	Yes	12 self-insured, 9 fully insured	6	63	rate bands	no	none	elective small employer reinsurance program

	Definition of small group	Guaranteed issue all products	Guaranteed renewability	Preexisting condition exclusion limits (months)	Lookback period limits (months)	Maximum gap in prior coverage (days)	Rating restrictions	Standardized plans required?	Mini-COBRA coverage (months)	Other reforms
IA	2-50	Yes	Yes	12	6	63	rate bands	no	9	elective small employer reinsurance program
KS	2-50	Yes	Yes	12 self-insured, 90 days fully insured	6	63	rate bands	no	6	mandatory small employer reinsurance program
KY	2-50	Yes	Yes	12	6	63	rate bands	yes, other plans permitted	18	
LA	2-50	Yes	Yes	12	6	63	rate bands, groups of 3-35	no	12	
ME	1-50	Yes	Yes	12	6	63 self-insured, 90 fully insured	modified community rating	yes, other plans permitted	12	small group carriers permitted to form reinsurance pool after state has approved their proposal
MD	2-50, 1 for g-issue during open enrollment	Yes	Yes	12 self-insured, 0 fully insured and HMOs	6	63	modified community rating	yes, riders may be added of which some are G-issue	18	hospital rate setting to control costs, elective small employer reinsurance program

MA	1-50, non-standard plans soon to be out of market	Yes	Yes	12 self-insured, 6 fully insured, 0 for HMO	6	63	modified community rating	yes, other plans permitted	18-36, special rules for divorced and separated spouses of fully insured plan members	mandatory small employer reinsurance program
MI	2-50 (as required by federal law)	Yes	Yes	12 self-insured, 0 HMOs & BC/BS	6	63	no restrictions,* except for Blue Cross Blue Shield, which community rate	no	none	
MN	2-50	Yes	Yes	12	6	63	rate bands	no	18	elective small employer reinsurance program
MS	2-50	Yes	Yes	12	6	63	rate bands	yes, for groups of 25 or smaller, other plans available	12	
MO	1-50	Yes	Yes	12; 0 if diagosis made but no treatment or advice provided in the last 12 months for groups over 25 only	6	63	rate bands for groups of 3-25	yes, for groups of 3-25; other plans permitted	9	elective small employer reinsurance program

	Definition of small group	Guaranteed issue all products	Guaranteed renewability	Preexisting condition exclusion limits (months)	Lookback period limits (months)	Maximum gap in prior coverage (days)	Rating restrictions	Standardized plans required?	Mini-COBRA coverage (months)	Other reforms
MT	2-50	Yes	Yes	12	6	63	rate bands	yes, other plans permitted	none	mandatory small employer reinsurance program, currently not accepting new enrollees and will be completely phased out by July 2001
NE	2-50	Yes	Yes	12	6	63	rate bands	no	6 for employees, 12 for spouses & dependents of deceased	mandatory small employer program
NV	2-50	Yes	Yes	12	6	63 self-insured, 90 fully insured	rate bands	no	18 for employees, 36 for dependents in some cases	elective small employer reinsurance program
NH	1-100	Yes	Yes	12 self-insured; 3 fully insured, if no claims in first 3 mos. of coverage; 9 fully insured, if claims made during first 3 mos.	6 self-insured, 3 fully insured	63	modified community rating	no	18	

NJ	2-50	Yes	Yes	12 self-insured, 6 fully insured groups of 2-5, 0 fully insured groups 6-50	6	63	modified community rating	yes, other plans permitted	12	
NM	2-50, 1 for self-employed people buying family coverage in the Alliance	Yes	Yes	12 self-insured, 6 fully insured	6	63	rate bands, modified community rating in Alliance	no	6	Health Insurance Alliance--purchasing group for small employers
NY	2-50	Yes	Yes	12	6	63	community rating	no	18-36	mandatory pooling program for small groups
NC	2-50, 1 for standard & basic plans	Yes	Yes	12	6	63	rate bands	yes, other plans permitted	18	elective small employer reinsurance program
ND	2-50	Yes	Yes	12	6	63	rate bands for 2-25; no restrictions for groups of 26 or more*	yes, other plans permitted	39 weeks	mandatory small employer reinsurance program
OH	2-50	Yes	Yes	12	6	63	rate bands	no	6, if employer has 10-19 employees	elective small employer reinsurance program

	Definition of small group	Guaranteed issue all products	Guaranteed renewability	Preexisting condition exclusion limits (months)	Lookback period limits (months)	Maximum gap in prior coverage (days)	Rating restrictions	Standardized plans required?	Mini-COBRA coverage (months)	Other reforms
OK	2-50	Yes	Yes	12	6	63	rate bands	no	30 day extension of fully insured plans	elective small employer reinsurance program
OR	2-50	Yes	Yes	12 self-insured, 6 fully insured	6	63	modified community rating for groups of 2-25	yes, other plans permitted	6	
PA	2-50	Yes	Yes	12	6	63	no restrictions,* BC/BS community rate as matter of practice	no	none	
RI	2-50, 1 for basic and economy plan	Yes	Yes	12	6	63	rate bands	yes, other plans permitted	18, but narrower than COBRA	elective small employer reinsurance program
SC	2-50 (including self-employed married couples)	Yes	Yes	12	6	63	rate bands	yes, other plans permitted	6	elective small employer reinsurance program
SD	2-50	Yes	Yes	12	6	63	rate bands	no	18 or 36	
TN	2-50	Yes	Yes	12	6	63	rate bands for groups of 3-25	no	3	elective small employer reinsurance program

TX	2-50	Yes	Yes	12	6	63; fully insured plans must credit all previous coverage during last 12 months even if there was a gap of more than 63 days	rate bands	no	6	elective small employer reinsurance program
UT	2-50	Yes	Yes	12	6	63	rate bands	no	6	
VT	1-50	Yes	Yes	12, 0 fully insured if 9 months creditable coverage	6	63 self-insured, 90 fully insured	community rating	yes, other plans permitted but must meet standards of common health plans	6	small group carriers must form state-approved reinsurance pool
VA	2-50	Yes	Yes	12	6	63	rate bands applied to the standard and essential plans; no reforms for other plans	yes, other plans permitted	none	
WA	1-50	Yes	Yes	12 self-insured, 9 fully insured	6	63 self-insured, 3 months fully insured	modified community rating	yes, other plans permitted	to be specified by insurer	
WV	2-50	Yes	Yes	12	6	63	rate bands	no	18	
WI	2-50	Yes	Yes	12	6	63	rate bands	no	18	
WY	2-50	Yes	Yes	12	6	63 self-insured, 90 fully insured	rate bands	no	12	mandatory small employer reinsurance program

* rates may still be subject to some level of state oversight, such as requirement that rates be actuarially justifiable.

APPENDIX 3
Glossary of Terms

Activities of Daily Living: Everyday living functions and activities individuals perform without assistance. These functions include mobility, dressing, bathing, personal hygiene, and eating.

Assisted Living: A living arrangement wherein housing is offered, but coupled with various levels of continuing care, with the goal of encouraging residents to achieve and maintain their maximum level of independent function. These arrangements typically provide various levels of evolving care to meet the changing needs of individuals who reside within the facility, and the charges by the facility will depend upon the level of assistance services provided within the housing.

Capitation: An agreement between a payer and a health delivery network to deliver a set of services to enrollees for a fixed amount. The scope of services can range from preventive care and laboratory tests to hospital care to comprehensive health care. The payment is fixed regardless of the number of services rendered. May also be the basis for payment to individual providers. This is used, for example, in Health Maintenance Organizations.

Catastrophic health insurance plan: A health insurance plan with a low premium that will pay for specified medical benefits only after a high deductible has been met. (Also known as "excess health insurance.")

Coinsurance: The portion of health care costs a patient must pay even after a deductible is met. Also referred to as a "co-payment."

Community Rating: A methodology of setting insurance premiums on the average cost of an entire community's health experience rather than that of a specific group that may be either healthier or more at risk than the community as a whole.

Co-payment: The portion of health care costs a patient must pay even after a deductible is met. Also referred to as "coinsurance."

Custodial Care: Care ordered by a doctor to help individuals meet personal needs such as bathing, dressing, and eating. Care may be provided by someone without professional skills or training.

Deductible: The amount a patient pays before a third-party payer begins to pay toward the costs otherwise covered under the plan.

Employee Retirement Income Security Act (ERISA): A 1974 federal law designed to protect employee benefits. It exempts companies that self-insure their enrollees' benefit programs from complying with state insurance laws and regulations; through federal preemption, it also prevents enrollees from utilizing state insurance legal remedies to challenge employer-sponsored plan decisions.

Endowment Life Insurance: A life insurance policy that pays a sum or income to the policyholder if the policyholder lives to a certain age. If the policyholder dies before that age, the policy pays a death benefit to the beneficiary. This insurance develops cash values over time.

Exclusive Provider Organization (EPO): A stringently-defined managed care plan with an exclusive list of providers and no out-of-network benefits. These plans typically have a limited number of providers, heavy utilization controls, and limited network EPOs are more likely to provide cheaper premiums and better control of expenditures, but with significant limits on flexibility and choice.

Experience Rating: The process of determining insurance premium rates based on the experience of a specific group, such as a specific company, union or professional group, rather than a community as a whole.

Fee-for-service: The traditional financing arrangement between providers and payers under which payment is based on what the provider charges for individual health care services. These plans allow you to select your own physicians, hospitals and other health care providers. You will generally have a deductible to meet and then eligible services are covered at a percentage of costs. This type of plan allows you significant flexibility but requires that you pay certain out of pocket expenses. Generally, the health care provider is reimbursed directly by the insurance company after services have been rendered. See also **traditional indemnity carriers**.

Formulary: A list of items approved for payment. A drug formulary, for example, is a restrictive list that limits payment for certain drug therapies unless physicians are able to obtain additional approval. Formularies may also be used for durable medical equipment.

Freedom of choice: The ability of consumers to select or change their own doctors. Also the ability of a consumer to go directly to a specialist without seeking referral from primary care physicians.

Gatekeeper: A primary care physician responsible for coordinating all services for a patient in a managed care plan. Generally, in order for specialty and hospital care to be covered, the gatekeeper must first approve the referral.

Group coverage: Groups of individuals, such as employees of corporations, union members, and members of professional or fraternal associations, who are insured as a unit. The sponsoring organization can usually negotiate discounts on the groups' premiums.

Guaranteed cost: A life insurance policy in which every feature is fixed so that the future costs can be ascertained with certainty in advance. Like nonparticipating policies, guaranteed cost policies do not accrue dividends. See **Nonparticipating policy**.

Guaranteed issue: An insurance plan that a sponsoring organization guarantees will be issued upon application by a qualified organization member, with premiums charged at the ordinary group rates, regardless of the health status of the applicant.

Guaranteed renewability: The assurance that an insurance company will continue to offer a policy to an individual or group that has made premium payments on a timely basis. An insurance company could not drop coverage due to specific circumstances, including high medical claims or illness. However, the insurer can raise premium rates if it does so for all policies in a certain class, after approval by the state insurance department.

Health Maintenance Organization (HMO): Health plan that combines an insurance system with a delivery system to finance and provide care to individual members. Payment is capitated and benefits for members are defined. These plans provide comprehensive health care services to their subscribers through the utilization of pre-determined and pre-approved facilities and health care providers. Unlike traditional indemnity plans, when you enroll in an HMO plan you a responsible for a very small out of pocket amount, and you have no deductible unless you go outside the plan's approved provider network. This type of plan provides less flexibility and freedom to choose your health care provider, unless you are willing to pay more. Except in very limited circumstances, HMOs do not cover services delivered by providers who are not participating in the plan. Members typically choose a primary care physician, known as a gatekeeper, responsible for all referrals regarding the patient's care.

Individual coverage: Insurance purchased by a single person rather than a group. Individual coverage may be difficult and costly to obtain for individuals with pre-existing conditions. See **pre-existing condition exclusion**.

Intermediate Care: Occasional nursing and rehabilitative care ordered by a doctor and performed or supervised by skilled medical personnel.

Job lock: The inability of an individual to change employers for fear of losing health coverage, particularly if the employee or a dependent has a pre-existing condition. See **pre-existing condition exclusion**.

Level premium: Regardless of age or changes in health, the premium paid when an individual first qualifies for coverage will never increase. Premium adjustments may be made only to an entire group of people in a given state and only upon 30 days' advance notice.

Long-term care: A comprehensive range of health, social and support services to meet the needs of people who have a condition or disability that is expected to be of long duration. Can be provided in the home, a retirement community, a nursing home or other facility.

Managed care: A broad term used to describe (1) organizations that combine financing and delivery of health care services, such as an HMO or PPO and (2) techniques used to control costs and utilization (e.g., utilization review, prior authorization). See **Health Maintenance Organization, Preferred Provider Organization, Prior authorization,** and **Utilization review**.

Medicaid: A federal-state program to finance acute and long-term care services for certain categories of poor and low-income individuals – primarily families with dependent children, the elderly and the disabled.

Medical savings account (MSA): An individual savings account where deposits are excluded from an individual's taxable income and withdrawals from the account are tax free if the money is used to pay for medical expenses.

Medicare (Part A/Part B): A federal program that finances medical care for people age 65 and older and for certain disabled individuals under age 65. Part A covers inpatient hospital, home health, hospice and limited, skilled nursing home services. Beneficiaries must pay deductibles and co-payments. Part B covers physician, outpatient laboratory and X-ray test, durable medical equipment, outpatient hospital care and certain other services. Part B is a voluntary program that requires beneficiaries to pay a monthly premium, as well as deductibles and coinsurance.

Medicare managed care plan: A Medicare approved network of doctors, hospitals, and other health care providers that agrees to give care in return for a set monthly payment from Medicare. A managed care plan may be any of the following: a Health Maintenance Organization (HMO), Provider Sponsored Organization (PSO), Preferred Provider Organization (PPO), or a Health Maintenance Organization with a Point of Service Option (POS). An HMO or a PSO usually asks you to use only the doctors and hospitals in the plan's network. If you do, you may have little or no out-of-pocket cost for covered services. A PPO or POS usually lets you use doctors and hospitals outside the plan for an extra out-of-pocket cost.

Medicare medical savings account: A health insurance policy with a high yearly deductible coupled with a Medicare-provided medical savings account. This is a test program currently. Medicare pays the premium for the Medicare MSA Plan and deposits money into a separate Medicare MSA you establish. You use the money in the Medicare MSA to pay for medical expenses. You can accumulate money in your Medicare MSA to pay for extra medical costs. Your insurance policy has a high deductible. There are no limits on what providers can charge you above what is paid by your Medicare MSA Plan.

Medicare private fee-for-service plan (PFFS): A Medicare-approved private insurance plan. Medicare pays the plan a premium for Medicare-covered services. A PFFS Plan provides all Medicare benefits. The PFFS Plan (rather than Medicare) decides how much to pay for the covered services you receive. Providers may bill you more than the plan pays (up to a limit) and you must pay the difference. It is likely that you will pay a premium for a PFFS plan.

Medicare supplemental insurance: A private insurance policy that meets federal standards for supplementing Medicare benefits. Such policies typically reduce deductibles and coinsurance on Medicare-covered services but may also cover benefits not available under Medicare (e.g., **outpatient** prescription drugs). Medicare supplemental insurance is also referred to as Medigap insurance.

Medigap insurance: See **Medicare supplemental insurance**.

Multiemployer welfare arrangement (MEWA): a plan whereby a number of small employers group together, and use combined premiums and joint administration to provide insurance coverage. These plans are established by trade associations and other entities and offered to small employer groups. The employers themselves are supposed to pay the medical bills. If there's an insurance company involved, it is only administering the plan. In the past, some MEWAs have set premiums too low to cover future claims. If they fail, you're stuck with any outstanding medical bills.

Noncancelable: Policies that have fixed premiums throughout the life of the contract. When you buy such a policy you are assured that your premiums will never rise.

Nonforfeiture Benefits: This clause applies where, for one reason or another, an insured stops making payments on their insurance policy. A nonforfeiture benefit is a form of a cash value that is paid up during the life of the policy. An alternative kind of provision is a "return of premium" benefit rider that offers a partial return of premium if the insured dies or the policy is dropped before any benefits are received.

Nonparticipating policy: A life insurance policy for which the insurance company does not pay dividends to the policyholder. See also **Guaranteed cost policy**.

Open enrollment: A limited period of time during which insurers accept any individual seeking coverage regardless of medical history.

Participating policy: A life insurance policy for which the insurance company pays dividends to the policyholder.

Point-of-service (POS) plan: A modified managed care plan that allows enrollees to seek care from a non-plan provider at an added cost to the patient. See **Managed care. Compare to Exclusive Provider Organization**.

Portability: The ability of an individual to leave an employer's group health plan and obtain from the same insurer an individual policy not tied to the employment that could go with the employee instead of being tied to the prior employment, to avoid being denied coverage for a pre-existing condition. See **Pre-existing condition exclusion**.

Pre-existing condition exclusion: An exclusion used by insurers to avoid paying for care to treat a medical disease or condition that was or could have been diagnosed before enrollment under the new policy.

Preferred Provider Organization (PPO): Preferred provider organizations are a group of physicians, hospitals, clinics or home care professionals that contract with an insurance provider or employer to deliver health care services to subscribers at a discounted or pre-determined rate. Under a PPO, a subscriber can go out of network to receive health care services, and the PPO will pay for these services. However, the level of reimbursement for out of network services can be significantly less. PPO's are a cross between the traditional indemnity plan and the HMO. PPO's allow the subscriber the freedom and flexibility to choose their health care professional while controlling costs through special arrangements between the PPO and the participating provider. If your health care professional is a participating provider within the PPO organization, you receive better reimbursement for the services than if your physician were not participating in the network.

Prior authorization: The approval a provider must obtain from an insurer or other entity before performing certain procedures, using certain medical products or admitting a patient electively, in order for the service to be covered under the plan.

Respite Care: This is care provided to enable to caretaker to take a "break."

Self-insured plan: An employer-based benefits plan through which the employer, rather than an insurer, assumes the risk for the cost of services inclurred by its workers and their dependents. Under ERISA, such plans are exempt from state insurance law and regulation, allowing employers more freedom in selecting the benefits for which they will pay and exempting them from the liability of certain state taxes. Self-insured employers typically use a commercial insurer or third-party administrator to administer their benefit plan including claim payments. See **Employee Retirement Income Security Act**.

Skilled Care: Daily nursing and rehabilitative care ordered by a doctor and performed or supervised by skilled medical personnel.

Sheltered Care: Care provided in a living arrangement whereby staff provides support, assistance with meal preparation, appointments, shopping and other issues that might otherwise create an impediment to independent living arrangements. Note: these arrangements are typically used for adults with severe learning disabilities or mental health problems.

Term Life Insurance: A life insurance policy that provides a death benefit for a "term" of one or more years. Death benefits will be paid only if you die within that term of years. A common policy period would be one year, five years, ten years, or until the insured reaches age 65 or 70. It does not build up any of the nonforfeiture benefits or values associated with whole life policies.

Third-party payer: An insurance company or other entity that pays the cost of medical benefits on behalf of a patient.

Traditional indemnity carriers: The traditional financing arrangement between providers and payers under which payment is based on what the provider charges for individual health care services. These plans allow you to select your own physicians, hospitals and other health care providers. You will generally have a deductible to meet and then eligible services are covered at a percentage of costs. This type of plan allows you significant flexibility but requires that you pay certain out of pocket expenses. Generally, the health care provider is reimbursed directly by the insurance company after services have been rendered. See also **Fee-for-service**.

Underwriting: The process insurers use to determine whether they will accept an individual's or small group's application for insurance and on what basis. Consideration may be given to factors affecting risk, including pre-existing conditions, age, occupation, etc.

Universal Life Insurance: This is a form of life insurance, the hallmark of which is flexibility. Premium payments can be skipped, you can increase or decrease the face amount, lengthen or shorten the protection period, increase or decrease the premiums, change the premium paying period, and contribute or withdraw lump sums.

Usual, customary, and reasonable: an amount for a medical service that is considered a reasonable average for a geographic area. These amounts are reported by national consulting firms. Often referred to as "UCR."

Utilization review: A tool used by providers, health care organizations, and insurance companies to influence the use of health care resources with the objective of containing costs.

Variable Universal Life Insurance: This is like Universal Life Insurance, but the policy ties your death benefit and cash value to the investment performance of the securities in which your policy is invested, and you choose what your policy will be invested in. These policies give you a shot at higher growth.

Waiting Period: This is the time (typically 30, 60, or 90 days) during which your insurance policy provides no coverage, and you will be required to pay all expenses. This is common, for example, in disability and long term care policies.

Waiver of premium; After becoming disabled (disability or life insurance) or receiving care for a period of time (long-term care), as requirements are defined by policy, premiums due will be automatically paid for the insured by the insurance company.

Whole life insurance: A life insurance policy that gives death protection for as long as you live. These policies develop cash values that can be used to purchase additional continuing insurance protection, or form a basis for a collateralized loan from the insurance company, or that may be obtained in cash if the policy is surrendered.

APPENDIX 4
Social Security Retirement

When You Can Receive Full Benefits

Year of Birth	Age Years	Plus Months
pre-1938	65	0
1938	65	2
1939	65	4
1940	65	6
1941	65	8
1942	65	10
1943–1954	66	0
1955	66	2
1956	66	4
1957	66	6
1958	66	8
1959	66	10
1960 and later	67	0

How Earlier Retirement Will Reduce Your Benefits

Months Early	% of Full Benefit	Months Early	% of Full Benefit
2	98.9	32	82.2
4	97.8	34	81.1
6	96.7	36	80.0
8	95.6	38*	79.2
10	94.4	40*	78.3
12	93.3	42*	77.5
14	92.2	44*	76.7
16	91.1	46*	75.8
18	90.0	48*	75.0
20	88.9	50*	74.2
22	87.8	52*	73.3
24	86.7	54*	72.5
26	85.6	56*	71.7
28	84.4	58*	70.8
30	83.3	60*	70.0

As retirement age rises to +67, these early retirement percentages will apply.

APPENDIX 5
Insurance Rating Systems

Rank Number	A.M. Best	Standard Poors	Moody's	Fitch	Weiss
1	A++	AAA,AAAq	Aaa	AAA	A+
2	A±	AA+	Aa1	AA+	A+
3	A	AA,Aaq	Aa2	AA	A–
4	A–	AA–	Aa3	AA–	B+
5	B++	A+	A1	A+	B+
6	B+	A,Aq	A2	A	B–
7	B	A–	A3	A–	C+
8	B-	BBB+	Baa1	BBB+	C+
9	C++	BBB,BBBq	Baa2	BBB+	C–
10	C+	BBB–	Baa3	BBB–	D+

Lower ratings not included. The ratings are not necessarily equivalent in each rank.

INDEX

Note: Italic *f* indicates that term is found in a footnote.